Human Rights
in Post-Mao China

Westview Special Studies

The concept of Westview Special Studies is a response to the continuing crisis in academic and informational publishing. Library budgets are being diverted from the purchase of books and used for data banks, computers, micromedia, and other methods of information retrieval. Interlibrary loan structures further reduce the edition sizes required to satisfy the needs of the scholarly community. Economic pressures on university presses and the few private scholarly publishing companies have greatly limited the capacity of the industry to properly serve the academic and research communities. As a result, many manuscripts dealing with important subjects, often representing the highest level of scholarship, are no longer economically viable publishing projects-- or, if accepted for publication, are typically subject to lead times ranging from one to three years.

Westview Special Studies are our practical solution to the problem. As always, the selection criteria include the importance of the subject, the work's contribution to scholarship, and its insight, original- ity of thought, and excellence of exposition. We accept manuscripts in camera-ready form, typed, set, or word processed according to specifications laid out in our comprehensive manual, which contains straightforward instructions and sample pages. The responsibility for editing and proofreading lies with the author or sponsoring institution, but our editorial staff is always available to answer ques- tions and provide guidance.

The result is a book printed on acid-free paper and bound in sturdy, library-quality soft covers. We manufacture these books ourselves using equipment that does not require a lengthy make-ready process and that allows us to publish first editions of 300 to 1000 copies and to reprint even smaller quantities as needed. Thus, we can produce Special Studies quickly and can keep even very specialized books in print as long as there is a demand for them.

About the Book and Authors

The concept of individual human rights in the People's Republic of China, as in all communist countries, is fundamentally different from that in the West. Even so, the record of the Mao Zedong years is generally acknowledged as dismal even in China. This book investigates human rights in China from a historical perspective but concentrates on the period since the death of Mao in 1976. The authors analyze legal practices and institutions, intellectual and ideological policies, and economic changes implemented under the Deng leadership in order to evaluate the degree to which there have been real changes in the Chinese attitude toward human rights. They also examine the inherent conflicts between policies of modernization--which include increasing intellectual and material contacts with the West--and policies of limited individual freedoms typical in communist societies. An appendix analyzing over 2300 cases of arrests highlights the human rights condition in China today.

John F. Copper is Stanley J. Buckman Professor of International Studies at Rhodes College. He is the editor of Communist Nations' Military Assistance (Westview, 1983). Franz Michael is professor emeritus at George Washington University, where he was associate director and director of the Institute for Sino-Soviet Studies from 1964-1972. Dr. Michael's publications include Rule by Incarnation: Tibetan Buddhism and Its Role in Society and State (Westview, 1982). Yuan-li Wu is a professor of economics at the University of San Francisco and a consultant at the Hoover Institution.

Human Rights
in Post-Mao China

John F. Copper, Franz Michael,
and Yuan-li Wu

Westview Press / Boulder and London

Westview Special Studies on East Asia

Copyright © 1985 by Westview Press, Inc.

Published in 1985 in the United States of America by Westview Press, Inc.,
5500 Central Avenue, Boulder, Colorado 80301; Frederick A. Praeger,
Publisher

Library of Congress Catalog Card Number: 84-52862
ISBN: 0-8133-0182-3

Printed and bound in the United States of America

10 9 8 7 6 5 4 3 2 1

Contents

Tables

Preface

For several decades little has been said about the human rights situation in China. There was no detailed analysis of China's human rights record published. One reason was that little was known about the subject; there was little information published in China and foreign scholars were not allowed to observe, much less study, the human rights condition in situ. In addition, many foreign scholars were friendly toward the government of the People's Republic of China, and, hence, avoided the subject both in public discussions and in research. Others felt that attracting attention to the subject would adversely affect China's relations with the United States and other Western nations and for that reason eschewed the topic. Still others felt that the Soviet Union deserved criticism, not China, and preferred to publicize Moscow's failings and not make comparisons which might appear to soften the Kremlin's culpability.

China's human rights situation clearly deserves greater attention, probably more than any nation on the face of the earth. First, there are more humans there whose rights can be violated or preserved. Second, China is opening to the rest of the world and its human rights situation, which has been and still is a topic that is carefully avoided, cannot be hidden forever. Discussion of it certainly cannot remain indefinitely taboo. Third, China's human rights condition is one of the least understood of the more than one hundred sixty nations of the world community. Finally, since a common argument is that China's human rights situation has improved, what that means or whether it indeed is true deserves a closer look. Since China accounts for nearly a fourth of humankind, it would be difficult to state with honesty that the world's human rights situation has improved if China's has worsened.

The analysis jointly undertaken by the authors is to some extent, perhaps a large extent, colored by "Western bias." The authors readily admit this. U.N. human rights documents are also "biased" in this sense. Yet they are signed and endorsed by a large majority of the member nations of the United Nations. These documents are Western in origin in terms of their intellectual and legal content as is the concept of human rights itself. Still individual freedoms, rights, opportunities, happiness and livelihood are of central concern in almost all societies. Moreover, China is also being treated by other standards that are of Western origin: economic growth, to give but one example.

The authors wish to thank a number of other scholars for their comments, ideas and input. None will be mentioned by name since they are too numerous. Special thanks are due, however, to Jan Chen, C.C. Wang and Y.H. Wu for their assistance in data gathering and evaluation. Mistakes are to be blamed solely on the three names on the cover.

It is the authors' hope that this study of China's human rights will contribute to an understanding of China and the global human rights problem. It is also hoped that by assessing and publicizing China's human rights situation more will be known in the West about China's problems, present condition, and prospects, as well as the true character of Chinese traditional culture. May this lead to an improvement in the freedoms and rights, not to mention hopes and aspirations, of more than a billion fellow human beings.

A final note: Throughout this book, the Pinyin system is used in the transliteration of Chinese proper names for persons, places and publications that are in a current People's Republic context. We have, however, retained either the Wade-Giles system or traditional spelling in all other situations because of their long-standing usage. Lastly, whenever the words "Communist Party" or "Communist" are capitalized, we have in mind specifically the Chinese Communist Party.

John F. Copper
Franz Michael
Yuan-li Wu

1
Introduction

> Economic growth and human progress
> make their greatest strides when
> people are secure and free to
> think, speak, worship, choose their
> own way and reach for the stars.

President Reagan spoke these words in Peking during his
visit to the People's Republic of China in April 1984.
The President's statement created more than a little
stir among some of his hosts who had to decide whether
their promised broadcast of the President's speech
should include this American statement on Human Rights.
Historically we can trace these ideas to the U.S.
Declaration of Independence:

> We hold these truths to be self-
> evident, that all men are created
> equal, that they are endowed by
> their creator with certain unalien-
> able rights, that among these are
> Life, Liberty and the Pursuit of
> Happiness--that to secure these
> rights, governments are instituted
> among men, deriving their just
> powers from the consent of the
> governed.

These revolutionary ideas had their echo through Europe
and, indeed, the world.
The American Revolution had its impact on France.
In fact, it inspired the French Revolution. The French
slogans of Liberty, Equality and Brotherhood in turn
expand on the American aspirations for human freedom.
Subsequently, to guarantee these principles and a
concept of human rights, Americans adopted the Bill of
Rights as a part of their new Constitution.
More than a century later the Wilsonian concept of
self-determination was embodied in the Covenant of the
League of Nations and began to internationalize the

1

concept of people's rights. It was World II, however, that reintroduced, in answer to Hitler's totalitarianism, the rights of the individual person as a human being. President Roosevelt, struggling with the problem of defining the free world's goals, proclaimed the "Four Freedoms": Freedom of Speech, Freedom of Religion, Freedom from Fear and Freedom from Want. These, he said, are the basic rights of all people. The essence of these ideas was accepted by the international community and incorporated in the United Nations Charter and reaffirmed and expanded in the Universal Declaration of Human Rights of December 10, 1948. Set forth in 30 articles, these rights are all inclusive. The Universal Declaration was subsequently supplemented by two Covenants, the International Covenant on Economic, Social and Cultural Rights and the International Covenant on Civil and Political Rights, and an Optional Protocol, all of 1966.

In their conceptual evolution these rights were regarded as absolutes endowed to all human beings. They were natural rights, not rights granted by the state or any other collective authority. They were asserted by the individual and confirmed by the community. Statecraft, therefore, is intended to reinforce and protect these rights. Although the several U.N. documents are only recommendations and in many cases not ratified by individual member governments of the United Nations, they nevertheless constitute the heart of the Human Rights issue.

In Western tradition, the creation and guaranteeing of human rights is accomplished in four ways: 1. Building a system of law fundamental to the precepts of fairness and respect of each individual as a human being in an organized society. This has served the purpose of guaranteeing individual freedoms while regulating human relations. Protection under law, therefore, is a basic right. 2. Encouraging and facilitating the participation of the people in the decisions of their government, originally directly and later through a form of representation. This is the basic human right that constitutes democracy. 3. Providing for the individual's economic freedom of choice without which other rights are vulnerable. This forms the material basis of human rights. 4. Protecting the freedom of the mind, including the right to peaceful communication of thoughts and beliefs. This assures the fullest development of the individual and of society as a whole.

This system of individual rights described above possesses a humanist quality and a moral foundation.

Its emphasis on the individual's rights and the very concept of such rights are of comparatively recent origin in human history. They have emerged out of human ethics. They have grown with the popularization of democracy and in reaction to dictatorships and totalitarian systems. A system of human rights is also seen by many as a sine qua non for the success of internationalism in a peaceful world. Thus in spite of the differences of the world's great cultures, East and West, it is presumed that basic common denominators of ethics can be found on which a modern universal concept of human rights can be built and made operational.

But the common ground of human ethics has not proved to be entirely firm. The total defeat of a most virulent form of totalitarianism and militarism, both West and East, in World War II did in fact create an atmosphere of optimism in the Western world that the time had come to establish the concept of human rights on an international scale. It was in this milieu that the newly founded United Nations issued its Universal Declaration of Human Rights. Not long afterwards, however, it became apparent that this aspiration, which was so ardently favored in the West, was not shared by all governments throughout the world. The Soviet Union and the newly founded communist countries, although outwardly going along with the general temper of the time, harbored quite different ideas on the individual's role in society and state. Similarly the newly independent nations and many developing countries had priorities that stressed improvements in economic and social conditions before the rights of the individual in society. This matter of priority became evident in United Nations' debates on the 1966 covenants. To the communist countries and much of the Third World the newly stressed rights were seen as national rather than individual. They were interpreted to mean self-determination and the right to protect each sovereign country's use of its natural wealth and resources. Nevertheless it was expressly stated in the U.N. documents that the so-called national rights should not encroach on the basic, political, social, cultural and economic human rights as existing or agreed to in each country.[1]

Far more serious, however, is the unwillingness of communist nations to apply in earnest what they had nominally agreed to. Nor have the differences in the usage of such terms as "democracy" or "general welfare" been resolved or even fully exposed. According to the Marxist-Leninist interpretation of history, society advances through class struggle. The state is the coercive instrument of the ruling class which governs through dictatorship. In the final stage of this inexorable process, the proletariat, an alleged majority, establishes its "dictatorship" over the rest of society (not directly, but through the intermediary of a "vanguard," the Communist Party). Accordingly, human rights as individual rights are inherently ruled out. The whole conceptual framework of classes, of dictatorship, of an elite vanguard, and of class

struggle precludes any equal treatment of individuals
qua individuals.

This conceptual framework fosters special powers
and privileges for the members of the vanguard. Even
the practice of "democratic centralism"--according to
which everyone participates in debating an issue, but
has to obey without reservation the decision of the
leadership--applies only to the so-called "vanguard."
Disagreement outside the vanguard becomes "counter-
revolutionary" and is to be suppressed. In reality the
privileged position of the members of the Party and
particularly of the leader of the "vanguard" results
inevitably in exploitation and the exercise of arbitrary
power and in oppression beyond the dicta of the doctrine
which already excludes the protection of individual
rights in the traditional sense.

Morever, the goal of the transformation of the
society means that individual rights can be and are
readily sacrificed. Since social change becomes a
paramount goal, as it does in communist nations, the
society is by definition put above the individual. The
need to eliminate enemy classes and to keep the
dictatorship intact makes sacrifices of the individual
inevitable. In each case of a communist takeover since
the Bolshevik revolution, class struggle has resulted in
large scale liquidation of "enemy" classes--usually
after the seizure of power and with a very large loss of
life. For the Marxist-Leninists this is necessary to
attain the final goal of an ideal social order. Still
communist leaders and revolutionaries are willing to pay
lip service to Western concepts of human rights when it
suits their purpose. This occurs most often when world
public opinion is a matter of concern to them. But
their genuine view is opposed to the individuals' rights
which they regard as capitalist in origin and obstruc-
tive to communist goals.

Nowhere is this more clearly expressed than in an
article in Renmin Ribao (People's Daily) on April 13,
1982, entitled, "The History and Present Condition of
Human Rights." Going back to the Declaration of
Independence and the French Revolution and calling on
Karl Marx as a qualified witness, the author labels all
human rights declarations up to the Covenants of 1966 as
"capitalist documents" dealing with the "rights of the
capitalist class." Only the "right to development" of
the formerly colonial and dependent countries can
"translate human rights on paper to real human rights."
Aside from this, human rights have been used by the
Soviet Union, the United States and the European
countries simply as a "tool" in propaganda attacks upon
one another. As far as the writer was concerned, the
People's Republic of China was a developing nation and
therefore qualified to claim being a champion of these
"new" human rights. Referring to basic rights as listed

in the latest Chinese constitution and claiming both
socialist and developing country status, the author in
Renmin Ribao asserts:

> Our public ownership of the means
> of production and our system of
> reward according to work, our
> system of the National People's
> Congress, our socialist democracy
> and our socialist legal system have
> given rise to a new form of
> safeguard for human rights in their
> economic, political and legal
> aspects.

Thus Marxism-Leninism Chinese style is also philosophically in disagreement with the Western principles
of human rights. Society's interest is primary, but
society's interest is realized only through the Party
and, in effect, the Party's leadership. Society is not
seen as a voluntary, cohesive group, but as sharply
divided into classes. Rights are not endowed by nature,
but depend on class status and are granted by leaders
whose interpretation of society's interest determines
what rights can be given at any specific time and to
whom. Rights given today can be taken away tomorrow in
accordance with changing circumstances and a changing
party line. Rights are maintained only by the pretense
that the party line requires their maintenance, for the
party line at any given time is the "truth" of that
time. In Marxism-Leninism the issue is not just
violations of human rights, violations which occur
unfortunately in any system, but rather the values of
the Marxist-Leninist system itself which constitute a
denial of human rights as we understand them.
    Given the theoretical as well as practical
incompatibility between Marxism-Leninism and the Western
tradition of human rights, the question we ask is
whether post-Mao China's new policies have fundamentally
affected the Chinese Marxist-Leninist view of individual
human rights. How do human rights actually fare in
post-Mao China? Has the human rights situation in the
People's Republic of China changed "for the better"?
    We ask these questions of post-Mao China only
partly out of intellectual curiosity. There are a
number of practical reasons besides, not the least of
which is the fact that in this country discussions on
human rights have invariably focused on the Soviet
Union. Since the People's Republic of China became
estranged from the Soviet Union in the 1960s while it
was still under Mao's rule, Western nations have at
times looked upon China as a nation that is of interest
almost exclusively because it is anti-Soviet and
therefore have downgraded the importance of how the

Chinese people have fared under communist rule. Moreover, following the death of Mao, there was a short period during the internal struggle for power in China when various freedoms appeared suddenly. The until then complete political control by the state and Party was loosened, which led some political observers to think that the prospects of political freedom might indeed be improving. We wish, therefore, to assess exactly how much and how permanently the human rights situation in China has really changed. For many of the freedoms and rights granted during Deng Xiaoping's rise to power have since been taken away.

After the overthrow of the Maoist radicals and the replacement of Hua Guofeng by Deng Xiaoping, de-Maoization went quite far, including the toppling of Mao from his former oracular niche. Many questions were asked at that time: Would a non-Maoist but still communist China be better for human rights? Or will communism based on Marxist-Leninist doctrine be just as incompatible with individual rights in China as it is in the Soviet Union? Is China's democratic movement, which could be the basis of progress in freedom and human rights, going to be lasting, or will it again be suppressed as happened several times in the past during Mao's leadership. Was it really accurate to say as many Western analysts did, that China had made meaningful progress in human rights, and seemed to be on the right track?

Our reasons go further. Intent on revitalizing the communist economic system, Party leader Deng and his lieutenants, in particular, Premier Zhao Ziyang, have introduced many reforms that have strong "capitalistic" features. To some Western observers this seems to be the prelude to the resurgence of a market economy in China. Will the newly granted economic freedoms which seem to be necessary to the success of the current economic development plans be retained, and will this lead to an expanding scope of human rights? Or will the practice of economic reform be limited to serving the cause of efficiency but not individual freedom? The answer to this question is important because a totalitarian, non-communist system was known before World War II under the label of fascism. The consequence of the evolution of such a regime in China can be quite serious for the United States, the Soviet Union and the whole world.

Our most important reason for addressing the question of human rights in post-Mao China is that the issue affects more than one billion people or nearly a quarter of the human race. Are the rights of the Chinese as members of humanity violated or infringed by an ideology and a political system under which they must live? And what are the implications for the global human rights movement?

The remaining chapters of this book deal respectively with the humanist tradition of pre-communist China and the diametrically opposite nature of the Maoist period from the perspective of human rights, the political, legal and economic policies of the Chinese Communist Party and government and their methods of policy implementation insofar as human rights are affected, and post-Mao China's attitude toward the freedoms of thought and beliefs. In each case an effort is made to show what is said on paper or by PRC officials and Party leaders and what then actually takes place. Emphasis is on the post-Mao period; the Maoist period is referred to only to provide whatever background may be necessary and for proper comparison. A concluding chapter then summarizes and pulls these points together so as to enable us to draw conclusions on the human rights condition in post-Mao China and the prospects that face the Chinese people and the Chinese Community Party. An appendix at the end of the book contains the findings of a statistical analysis of actual practice of China's criminal justice system during 1978-83. This analysis is based on individual reports during this period about the arrests of 2,369 persons in two national and local newspapers which have been carefully combed for the study. These findings offer important additional corroborative evidence to the analytical account in the rest of the book.

ENDNOTES

1. See Article 5, paragraph 2 of the International
    Covenant on Economic Social and Cultural Rights in
    Everyone's United Nations, Its Structure and Activ-
    ities (New York: United Nations, 1968), 8th
    edition, Appendices, pp. 416-423.

2
Humanist Ethics
in Chinese History

There have been as many incidences of cruelty and man's inhumanity to man in China's recorded past as in Western history or for that matter in the history of any other civilization. Yet if civilizations are to be judged not pathologically, but by their value systems and goals, a study of China's history reveals a regard for humanity as profound as that of any other great culture. Without a doubt this can be the foundation on which modern concepts of human rights can be built.[1] It is instructive to remember this in view of the many terrible brutalities and enormous loss of life that occurred during the last decades in China.[2] Too often China's recent history of barbarism has been rationalized by the uninformed--some might say racist-- who claim that the traits and traditions of China's past condemned Chinese society to a systemic defect. Misunderstanding Chinese communism and ignorance of its effect on China must not be compounded by claims that human freedoms and rights must necessarily be ignored by China because of its historical culture and values.

Traditional Chinese society was humanist. Nothing is more erroneous and misleading than the often heard idea that the Chinese communist system of totalitarian control is simply an extension of imperial despotism, that Mao Zedong was just another emperor, that the foundation of modern communism was there all along and that indeed communism was "good in China."[3] The truth is that communism in China was superimposed on a humanist tradition that grew through several millenia of history. There was a short tumultuous attempt at nation-building during the early part of the century and before the Sino-Japanese War (1937-45) in which modern concepts of rule by law and a free market economy were to be fused with the ethics and values of the past. The question now is what is left of Chinese humanism after decades of battering by an antagonistic system.

The Genesis of a Humanist Tradition

Recorded history in China begins in the thirteenth

9

century before Christ, when the age of magic ended and
the age of reason began. In the place of sacrifices to
a clan deity a new concept was revered, the belief in an
abstraction, Heaven, interpreted as a moral universe. A
moral human order was part of this moral universe,
linked to it by the ruler who had to possess as his
sanction for rule certain moral qualifications giving
him the "virtue" to hold the "mandate of Heaven" and
rule mankind. But he had the right to rule only as long
as he possessed this mandate. The founders of this new
political philosophy or ideology fully accepted an
inevitability about this concept--that their own new
Chou Dynasty was eventually bound to fall, as would
other coming dynastic rules in a system of rising and
falling dynasties that has characterized Chinese
imperial history.4 This concept, simplistic as it
appears to the modern historian, served as a basic
safety valve for imperial governments in China and
assured that government did not exist for its own sake
or by any divine right, but for a moral purpose--that of
maintaining a moral human order in the moral universe.
For this the emperor was responsible not to the people
but to Heaven.

In essence this meant institutionalizing the
government's concern for the well-being of the people.
It was the people's discontent that the ruler had to
worry about. It was "the suffering of the people" that
provided the new rulers of the Chou Dynasty with the
claim to their right to overthrow the past government
and establish their own. In the founder's words: "I am
concerned only with Heaven and the people."5 The
"virtue" of the ruler had thus a concrete content, and
it was believed to be the voice of the people through
which Heaven spoke.

Six hundred years later this concept was to be
given its more specific scope and meaning. This was the
period of the "hundred schools of thought" when a
revolutionary transformation from a feudal to a
bureaucratic order led to a search for new answers to
the question of the meaning of organized human life.
The term "hundred schools" was a slogan meant to
indicate the large number of such rivaling schools, not
any count of those known to contemporaries or posterity.
However, they were of uneven influence and significance.
The most important by far was the school of K'ung Fu-
tzu, latinized Confucius, who lived from 551 to 479 B.C.
and whose teachings, especially about politics and
ethics, and their combination, became the basis for the
moral beliefs and the social and political order of
imperial times lasting until the twentieth century.

What Confucius provided was not a training course
in the practical art of government but education in a
set of moral values. He was especially concerned with
the education of the new bureaucrats of his time, the

chun-tzu (or gentlemen/scholars), who were to assume the responsibility of leadership in society and state, and for whom he was to proclaim moral standards which were to serve as a model for all. Among the precepts of his moral code the most intrinsic were the principles of "jen," a moral feeling towards other men, sometimes rendered as "humanism" or "humanity" and "i," integrity, a consciousness of moral obligation of one's own ethically right behavior. These qualities were to be developed in each person through education--a humanist rather than a professional education.

As for his own time, a time of general moral decline, when the social and political ethics of the past were disdained, the only remaining loyalties were those within the family. These Confucius stressed. Moreover, he expanded on them, adding to the family loyalties of children to parents--"filial piety"--of wives to husbands, among brothers and sisters, the loyalties among friends and finally, between subjects and ruler which, analogous to family relationships, should be based on loyalty and obedience on one side and care and responsibility on the other. The ruler was likened to the father of his little children. Through the practice of these loyalties and responsibilities in the family, society and state, peace would be re-established and harmony and stability restored.

Aside from the role of the ruler, the Confucian moral code was built on the example of those who became through their knowledge and practice of it the new bureaucratic elite. Their role in society and the state depended not on any aristocratic right of birth, but on their education in these Confucian tenets. In his sayings Confucius prescribed rules of behavior for this scholar-elite, asserting what they could and should do and what they should not do, contrasting their way of action to that of the low person who acted only from base instincts. Confucius held that man, good by nature, needed education to bring out these moral qualities. He said: "The noble man understands what is right; the inferior man understands what is profitable." And "The noble man makes demands on himself; the inferior man makes demands on others." Or: "The resolute scholar and humane person will under no circumstances seek life at the expense of his humanity; on occasion he will sacrifice his life to preserve his humanity." On the importance of education: "By nature men are pretty much alike, it is learning and practice that sets them apart." And in his most revolutionary formulation, discarding the aristocratic strictures of the past feudal order: "In education there are no class distinctions."[6]

These statements and many others made to rulers of states and to his students were collected by them in the Confucian Analects. Together with other classical sources of the time ascribed to Confucius, they became the core of the teaching of the Confucian school of literati. They were supplemented almost two hundred years later by the most brilliant of Confucian followers, Meng-tzu, latinized Mencius, who restated and added sophistication and system to the master's ideas.

In his teachings Mencius placed even greater emphasis on the importance of the well-being of the people in the scheme of the universal moral order. It was, therefore, the will of Heaven alone that gave the mandate to govern to the ruler. But Heaven "did not speak." It was the people's acceptance that confirmed or challenged the ruler's mandate. For as Mencius taught: "Heaven sees as the people see, Heaven hears as the people hear." In the order of importance of the affairs of the world: "The people rank the highest, the spirits of land and grain come next, and the ruler counts the least."[7]

It took another two hundred years before these concepts were accepted as the basis for the imperial education system, supported by gradually institutional-ized state examinations, and for the ethical foundation for imperial rule; the durability they provided was not for any specific dynasty's rule, but for the social order on which all dynasties were erected.

A Broader Spectrum of Intellectual Tradition

The Confucian tradition is therefore compatible with the modern notion of human rights as founded in the well-being of the people as individual moral beings. Other philosophical developments contributed further to the stream of Chinese intellectual tradition. Taoism with its intuitive grasp of the mysteries of the universe and its quasi-religious approach to the individual's aspirations of coming to terms with the riddle of existence remained an antidote to the con-straints created by Confucian moralizing and a safety valve against the moral pressures of the Confucian system.

More important still in its contribution to the institutions of the imperial system was the school of the legalists. This system was first introduced by the great unifier of the Chinese polity, Ch'in Shih-huang-ti, the First Emperor of Ch'in in the third century B.C. Legalist concepts, as proclaimed at the time, defined a law that was equal for all, binding on the law giver, protected against all tampering and "clear, easy to know, and strictly applied." It contained the most important basic legal principles as known to Western tradition. Yet it was a ruthless and harsh system, treating society as made up of potential criminals only. Moreover, it was hostile to all humanist strivings, to the arts and world of ideas, as they did not serve the simplistic statist purpose of power concentrated in the hands of the emperor. It provided a normative order, intent on establishing equality for all, doing away with the aristocratic privileges and the caste distinctions of the feudal order. Behind the ruthlessness of the law, however, there were no ethical principles; and in spite of its character, the law and the oppressive authority behind it, though at first accepted, soon became detested. As Confucius had earlier warned: "Lead the people by law and regulate them by penalties, and the people will try to keep out of jail, but will have no sense of shame. Lead the people by 'virtue' and restrain them by ethics ('li') and the people will have a sense of shame and moreover will become good."[8]

The Buddhist Impact: Compassion

Before modern times, only one foreign system of beliefs and values affected this native Chinese cultural tradition and affected it deeply. Confucianism had not dealt with the question of life after death. Family loyalty included ancestor worship; yet while demanding the ceremony of the communal meal at the ancestral tomb, Confucius left undecided the issue of the existence of a spiritual world. He asked for sacrifice to the spirits "as if they were present," limiting his concern to life on earth. Nor did Taoism, with its efforts to learn the secrets of immortality through magic, satisfy the human search for ultimate answers. In fact, none of the Chinese schools of thought provided for a religious faith. Thus the Chinese were all the more deeply affected by Indian Buddhism, a foreign faith that reached China during the first centuries after Christ.

The Buddhism that came to China via the caravan routes of Central Asia and by sea had already undergone evolutionary changes. Mahayana Buddhism, the branch that spread to China, placed its stress on faith rather than on prolonged religious study. It also recognized the role of saintly beings, Bodhisattvas, Kuan Yin in Chinese, beings who had reached enlightenment but voluntarily decided to be reborn in this world to contribute to the salvation of all sentient beings. Faith, compassion and the concern with human suffering were the chief emotions stressed by Buddhist teachings. At a time of chaos and political decline Buddhism spread to all of China, providing charity and consolation, affecting art and architecture, shaping the landscape with its statues, temples and pagodas, and providing a deeper meaning to human existence. Later excesses eventually led to persecution and Buddhism's political star declined; nevertheless Buddhism with its many sects and many more practitioners remained to provide a religious foundation to Chinese society, and profoundly affected Confucian philosophy. The slogan used by the scholar-elite which claimed to "carry the burden of the world on their shoulders" is traceable to the

Bodhisattva concept of Mahayana Buddhism.

A Moral Safeguard: Dualism Between State and Society

Thus Confucianism, enriched by Taoism, Buddhism, and other teachings, remained the basic philosophy of Chinese society and state. It assumed a dialetical relationship between the state under the rule of the emperor--who was all powerful as long as he held the Mandate of Heaven--and the society which was led by the scholar-elite with a monopoly on office holding, and which in its social role remained the custodian of the Confucian ethics that the emperor himself would disregard only at his peril. The dual authority of the emperor's state power and the scholar-elite's ideological hegemony provided a balance that guaranteed the durability of the Chinese imperial tradition (notwithstanding the rise and fall of dynasties) and the continuity of the social order. No imperial "despotism" could in the long run overcome the Confucian ethics.

The laws of the state, which were criminal laws only, remained a last resort for maintaining order. Social relations were determined through suasion under a social code, in Chinese "li," in practice the most important way in maintaining social harmony. This system with its great social mobility and absence of hereditary castes or classes had the respect for moral values and human ethics in which modern human rights could well be founded. The Confucian concepts of "jen" and "i"--the care for others based on one's own integrity are clearly the foundation for respect for human rights. The legal tradition existed in Chinese culture, providing formal guarantees for a much broader ethical code of internal discipline, the "li," with its strong basis in social tradition. The Heavenly Mandate was in concept a popular mandate, human morality being a crucial part of a moral universe. The tolerance and compassion of Buddhism added the religious experience and the sense of acceptance of religious freedom. The pluralism of philosophical thought and traditions was a fertile ground for freedom of the mind and intellectual development; the limited state provided great leeway for the development of human rights in society.

To recapitulate and in simpler terms, when the Confucian, legalist, Buddhist, and Taoist teaching are merged, we have a total system that corresponds closely to the foundations of modern human rights. The Confucian "Mandate of Heaven" corresponds to the popular mandate of democracy. The legalists' equality before the law provides a legal framework. Buddhist compassion safeguards the rights of the weak and social welfare. Taoist other-worldliness tempers moralization while Confucian tolerance, self-restraint, and moral obligation are meant to reduce litigation and, therefore, the role of the state as arbiter and guardian of the law.

Reform or Revolution

The question remains: Was Confucianism incapable of serving a transformed society with new political, social, economic and intellectual forms of modern life? During the last phase of imperial history the Confucian concepts had become ossified and the examination system produced mainly stereotypes rather than really able policy makers and administrators. When China confronted the Western powers and accepted what was called the unequal treaties, the young generation held the system responsible for China's humiliations at the hands of the West. There followed a twofold attack against the Confucian order: The revolution of 1911 abolished the concept of the Mandate of Heaven together with the Imperial system and established a republic, and the May 4th movement in 1919 struck against the Confucian family authority, especially the parental arrangement for marriages of sons and daughters.9 It was a revolt of the young generation against the stifling aspects of the morals of the past, expressed in a new literature, political demonstrations and a new life style in the Westernized cities. But even the new literature, which claimed to be what one of its leading spirits called "the Chinese renaissance," traced its assumed roots back to a broader Chinese tradition.

Not all the intellectual leadership of the time was ready to break with the Confucian system. At the turn of the century one attempt was made to establish a modern society based on equality, a modern economy, a modern educational system and a modern democratic representative order within the framework of a Confucian state and society. K'ang Yu-wei (1858-1927) is regarded as the last creative thinker in the Confucian tradition. He wrote about a utopian future human order based on equality which China was to join while contributing its Confucian cultural ethics. For a short time K'ang held high office under a young Manchu emperor. His immediate aim as a political reformer was a constitutional monarchy with mass education, freedom of opinion and popular representation. Economic development was to be based on the free development of commerce and industry, with government encouragement rather than control. But K'ang's impetuous "hundred days of reform" were defeated by conservative vested interests, and instead of evolutionary transformation the revolution ended the Manchu empire and produced a republic. Yet in spite of the repudiation of the imperial system and of parental authority, Confucian ethics survived.

The National Government's Policy: Modern Laws

After years of turmoil, when a National Government was established, the program of building a modern nation was linked with the cultural concepts of the past. The most important measures taken by the government in its plan of creating a modern polity was the promulgation of modern laws in the early 1930s. A civil code, patterned after the continental European law--the code Napoleon and the Swiss and German civil codes--became the foundation of modern Chinese society. A criminal code, several economic codes, codes of procedure, altogether over a hundred modern laws were promulgated and put in force in the decade from 1927 to 1937, before the long years of war with Japan, merging into World War II and the renewed civil war, precluded further progress. These laws served modern life; but they were also harmonized with Chinese cultural tradition by the law givers and by the decisions of the Chinese Supreme Court, of great significance for its effort to fit modern norms into the framework of the ethical concepts of the past. These laws also created the framework for a free enterprise system and for free enquiry in education and scholarship. They again contributed to the basis for modern human rights.

What was missing in this design for modern statehood was enough time to have the new measures take full effect. The emerging nation state had to deal in military terms with the incorporation of warlord territories, the internal opposition of communist rebellion and, finally and most perilously, with the aggression by Japan which was determined to prevent the success of an independent Chinese nation state.

Aside from this handicap of giving priority to the military there was in retrospect perhaps a more serious want in the social environment of the time which hindered the emergence of a free social order based on citizen participation in the political process. The prolonged existence of the treaty ports prevented the growth of a Chinese middle class. Living under the protection of foreign powers, businessmen were prevented from assuming a logical place in a fight for their share in political power. When special foreign rights were finally abolished in the midst of war, it was too late to affect the outcome of a struggle for political rights that had been superseded by the military issue for victory in a civil war.

Under the People's Republic

In 1949, when the People's Republic was established, a totally different set of political/ethical concepts was introduced. Marxism-Leninsim, a Western ideology, had nothing to do in terms of its origin with Chinese or any other non-Western cultural tradition. In fact, its teachings were in principle hostile to the very values on which Chinese culture--and for that matter Judeo-Christian culture--was founded. The idea of class struggle and of the dictatorship of whatever class or "dictatorship by the majority" is in direct conflict with the Confucian goal of social harmony and of the Buddhist ideal of compassion. The practices introduced under this system produced an unending, in fact, formalized violation of human rights contrary to the humanist Chinese tradition. This concept of a political party as the vanguard of a class which decided the fate of all is in direct contradiction to the principle of equality in the political process ensured through freedom of speech, assembly and general elections. "Democratic centralism," even if it were applied, is for the members of the Party only, and in practice, power is in the hands of a self-elected oligarchy and actually in the ever reappearing one-man leadership.

In China, under Mao Zedong, all this was magnified. In essence Mao was a Stalinist, and though sometimes jealous of Stalin's superior authority, from the outset followed closely the directions of the leader of the communist world movement. An often held mistaken view has it that, in contrast to Soviet Marxism-Leninism, Mao allegedly shifted from urban, "proletarian" revolution to "peasant revolution." Actually the shift--not to peasant rebellion, but to rural-based prolonged so-called "wars of national liberation"--was Lenin's and Stalin's invention, accompanied by the proper doctrinal propaganda. The statement "The most important task of the Chinese communist party is to win the peasant masses for active struggle on behalf of fighting slogans which link up political and economic demands comprehensible to and important to the peasantry" was not made by Mao, but by Stalin in March 1926 to the Comintern.[10]

Mao had to learn this Soviet strategy and doctrine. The so-called Thought of Mao Zedong is but a Chinese popularization of Marxist-Leninist and Stalinist writings and ideas, including the often quoted slogan, "Political power grows out of the barrel of the gun," which came from a Stalinist statement quoted by Mao.[11]

Mao's Policy

Mao's strategy of political control and rule included the communist measures of terror to maintain control of the Party and, after the seizure of power, in carrying out continuous communist revolution. The bloody purges within the Party carried out by Mao to establish and maintain his leadership during the war years at Yenan were rationalized by his claim to represent the right doctrinal line, a claim and method initiated by Stalin and applied within all communist parties. The technique of Mao's Cheng Feng (rectification) movement (1942-44) used the guise of an education campaign to combine an assertion of this ideological authority with an attack against his competitors among the party leaders. This technique reached its apogee 25 years later in the so-called Great Proletarian Cultural Revolution, and was at that time used not only against rival leaders but in the destruction of the Party structure itself. In 1942, Mao used his own speeches and those of loyal lieutenants, together with essays by Lenin, Stalin and other Comintern leaders, as a measuring rod to accept members of his team for the restructured Party and to purge whoever appeared to him dangerous or questionable. The claim of ideological correctness of the leader and of not only political but ideological "deviation" of the opponents of the Party has remained standard procedure down to the Party rectification drive under Mao's successors in 1983.

Shortly after the seizure of power in 1949, however, began the extensive social revolution with its destruction of all rights and freedoms and the introduction of a totalitarian order. Immediately after the founding of the People's Republic Mao abolished all existing laws and did not replace them (with the single exception of the introduction one year later of a communist marriage law which was in many ways less detailed and less advanced than had been the marriage stipulations of the preceding Nationalist code). The communist marriage law was promulgated in connection with "land reform" in the form of a political movement, and introduced in practice the necessity of party approval of marriage and politically contrived divorce leading to gross misuse by local cadres of their power. The final result was a huge number of suicides. Aside from this law, Mao attacked the existing order not by laws but by political drives that affected target groups and classes on a national scale. In his directives, Mao usually treated the target group in percentage figures, setting quotas for the percentage that should be prosecuted, found guilty and punished in varying degrees of harshness or leniency. The drives could be started, interrupted and abandoned as the political goal required. In short, Mao's style of political control required an enemy and he simply defined one by edict.

The Agrarian Reform Act promulgated in June 1950 divided the peasantry into landless peasants, poor peasants, middle peasants, rich peasants and landlords. It started with land distribution, but ended after 1951 in mass trials on often unproved charges and executions in an atmosphere of mass hysteria and fear. It was followed by the Counter-revolutionary Suppression Campaign to eliminate all political opposition with huge mass public trials in the cities. The Three Anti-Movement and the Five Anti-Movement were directed against former Kuomintang officials and the business class respectively. (See Chapter 3.) The Study Campaign for Ideological Reform, started in September 1951, was designed to teach the intellectuals "the ideology of the progressive elements of the working class, that is to say, the revolutionary theories of Mao Zedong, a product of Marxism-Leninism, and the actual practice of the Chinese revolution."[12] The methods of "struggle" meetings which the target often did not survive and of "criticism, self-criticism and confession" were designed to eradicate independent thought as the seed of possible opposition to the new regime.

These drives and similar measures of intimidation, including labor camps, and of torture created an atmosphere of fear and prompted compliance and the automaton-like repetition of slogans and of the line of the moment, that characterized the Chinese population under Mao's rule. It is still echoed in the panicky reaction of intellectuals to policy changes in the post-Mao era.

If perhaps somewhat more insidious in his methods and more costly in human lives than had been the model of Stalin's Russia, Mao's policy in China remained in tune with the Soviet leadership. Even today the picture of Stalin remains one of the four communist idols displayed on great occasions together with Marx, Engels and Lenin. Only in the last years of Mao's rule, after de-Stalinization had threatened Mao's position in China and the Sino-Soviet conflict had embittered relations between the two communist powers, had Mao gone on his own.

Only in the later stages of the Great Leap Forward and the Great Proletarian Cultural Revolution, both disasters for China in economic, educational and cultural terms, did Mao finally deviate from the official communist line. The Great Leap was an attempt at building "instant communism" and was condemned by Moscow. It ended with disastrous consequences in the loss of life and economic destruction. The Cultural Revolution was Mao's grandiose plan to destroy the Chinese Communist Party which had turned against him and to replace it with his own organization, first the Red Guards, and when they failed, by his own "proletarian" followers. He used the decimated Party, turning it into a Maoist Party based on a leader cult that far surpassed that of Stalin.[13] The result of the thirty years of Chinese communism under Mao has been a decline in all aspects of the economy, especially in agriculture, a great loss of life and a cultural desert. Today, the Chinese communist leadership admits that the Cultural Revolution and the Great Leap were unmitigated disasters. Since Mao's image could not be totally discarded, however, the "Gang of Four" became the scapegoat for mistakes and "abuses" of the past.

Maoist policy, however, has been abandoned. The new line is a return to more orthodox communism with a type of "New Economic Policy" added. It is most of all an attempt to get out of the deep hole into which Maoist utopian phantasies led China. Maoism is gone, but communism remains. The question unresolved is whether, with the sobering experience of the past, a communist regime, experimenting in many ways with unheard of "un-communist" economic policies, can and will tolerate a minimum of human rights without losing its grip on society. On the one hand, totalitarian political and doctrinal control appears wholly at variance with all human rights. On the other hand, the basic ethics on which human rights have been founded and which are the fruits of a long and rich cultural tradition must surely have remained in the subconsciousness, perhaps even consciousness, of the Chinese people.

ENDNOTES

1. As a general introduction to Chinese cultural history, see, for instance, C. P. Fitzgerald, China, a Short Cultural History, 3rd ed. (New York: Holt, Rinehart & Winston, 1961). Also, a monograph by Franz Michael, China Through the Ages, A Short Cultural History, in preparation, to be published by Westview Press, Boulder, CO, in 1985.

2. Ansley J. Coale of the National Academy of Sciences and Princeton University was reported by the Times-Tribune News Service to have said that Chinese census figures released on July 11, 1984 showed the loss of life in China due to food shortage during Mao's "Great Leap Forward" to be 27 million. The Peninsula Times Tribune (San Mateo, CA), July 11, 1984, p. A-7.

3. See the discussion in John King Fairbank, Chinabound: A Fifty-Year Memoir (New York: Harper & Row, 1982), p. 317.

4. Herrlee G. Creel, The Origins of Statecraft in China (Chicago: U. of Chicago Press, 1970), Vol. I. See also, De Bary et al, ed., Sources of Chinese Tradition (New York: Columbia U. Press, 1960), pp. 12-14.

5. Ibid.

6. From the Analects as quoted in de Bary, Sources of Chinese Tradition, pp. 25, 29, and 33.

7. Ibid, p. 110. These ideas are diametrically opposed to the Marxist-Leninist idea of a Communist Party vanguard that alone can pronounce the truth.

8. Ibid, p. 17.

9. Se Chou, Tse-tsung, The May Fourth Movement, Intellectual Revolution in China (Cambridge: Harvard U. Press, 1960 and Stanford, CA: Stanford U. Press, 1967).

10. See Jane Degras, ed., The Communist International, 1919-1943, 3 vols. (New York: Praeger, 1964), Vol. II, p. 279. See also Franz Michael, Mao and the Perpetual Revolution (Woodbury, NY: Barron's Educational Service, Inc., 1977), p. 17.

11. Ibid, p. 13.

22

12. Quoted in Michael, _Mao and the Perpetual Revolution_, p. 95. Original text from Robert J. Lifton, _Thought Reform and the Psychology of Totalism: A Study of "Brain Washing" in China_ (New York: Norton, 1961).

13. Michael, _Mao and the Perpetual Revolution_, pp. 147 and ff.

3
Human Rights in the Polity of
the People's Republic of China

Introduction

It is axiomatic that the form, size, style and nature of the political system of any country are relevant to the quality of human rights in that country.[1] It follows that the human rights condition in democratic and communist nations will differ. In a communist country, the very nature of its political system makes human rights in the Western tradition of less concern to its leaders. Accordingly, the human rights record of communist nations is dismal as a rule. However, in relative terms, human rights can fare somewhat better, or a great deal worse, in a communist system depending upon the nature and urgency of the political issues the leaders face at any time and the solutions they believe they have available.

Since the People's Republic of China is and professes to be a communist state, what is said of communist systems in general also applies to China. In fact, Chinese leaders have taken a line similar to other communist nations, arguing that the human rights campaign of the United States is a "hypocritical farce" by the very nature of the American society and that the bourgeois democratic notion of human rights is much too limited and disguises the oppression of the working class in capitalist nations.[2] (See Chapter 1.) Our task here is to assess the actual condition of human rights in China, the trends and changes that are apparent especially since the death of Mao and whether, how and to what degree the Chinese communist system denigrates human rights.

When the communist regime came to power in 1949, it assumed control over a China that was exhausted after long years of suffering from foreign and civil wars. There were centrifugal tendencies and to many Chinese and others communism had yet to prove itself in terms of effective leadership and the nature of its governance. As the leader of the Chinese Communist Party and government, Mao Zedong sought complete political control over the population. Following communist theory and practice, he established nationwide thought control and propaganda organizations and energetically continued "class struggle." He defined a portion of the population of the Chinese nations as "class enemies." In his own words, five percent of the people (over 25 million persons in the 1949 mainland Chinese population) were "reactionaries" and had to be deprived of their rights.[3] In this manner Mao justified his harsh policies and provided a predefined scapegoat in the event things went wrong.

Structure of the Political System

Mao applied the Marxist-Leninist system of political control according to the Soviet model wherein the Party--wellspring of ideology from which all political decisions emanate--is supreme and infallible. Membership in the Party was selective and determined by the leadership. The Party became an elite group--never exceeding four percent of the population in China--based upon its right to define and propagate ideology and make all important policy decisions according to ideological precepts. Both the government and the military were conceived as tools of the dictatorship of the proletariat and were therefore under total Party control. In fact, virtually all administrative positions were occupied by Party members. While the government, military, and Party hierarchies were in principle separate, interlocking or double appointments on a large scale assured tight Party control of policy and its execution.[4] When running efficiently, these centers of political power, acting in unison, gave the Party absolute control. Even after 1952 when political authority on the mainland had been consolidated, Mao kept the PLA on war-footing. He envisaged the nation remaining at war both with itself--that is, with "feudal" and "capitalist" tendencies within and other opposition to socialism--and with the "capitalist bloc" that was perceived as surrounding and threatening the People's Republic. The war status rationalized the maintenance of an extremely large standing army in terms of manpower and the preservation of the military's elite status and special prerogatives, which included better food, greater opportunities to travel, and material comforts and privileges for the soldiers' families.

The Party and the government provided a double-tracked bureaucracy and administrative system down to the lowest level, in the cities as well as in the countryside, greatly facilitating the intensive and all-pervasive control of all facets of the individual's life. Not only was the Party the initiator of key policy decisions but Party members became occupants of supervisory positions within the administration. Party members have thus been able to use the government as a pliant tool, including the institution of special campaigns and drives to carry out Party policy which have so vitally affected human rights.

The Political System and Human Rights

Such was the system Mao established. If one were to read the Party or the national constitutions, one might gain the impression that power both in the Party and in the country is broadly based and representative. The opposite, however, is true. Mao's system emphasized the concentration and centralization of power; this remains so. Real decisions are made by the Party and at the top. The decisions are then transmitted downward. Ordinary Party officials (e.g., county Party secretaries) have local authority but no say on policy, not to mention the public at large. At the apex of the Party is the Standing Committee (less than ten persons) of the Politburo. Meetings of this Standing Committee and of the Politburo are secret; even the time and place are not made public. The Central Committee of the Party--a considerably larger body of elite Party leaders --meets irregularly and usually simply approves and explains decisions already made at the top. The National Party Congress, a much larger body, meets even less regularly. When the latter body does convene, it is brought up to date on events and policies and essentially rubber stamps decisions already made by the Standing Committee of the Politburo, the Politburo itself, or the Central Committee.[6] Local Party organizations are supposed to provide feedback but generally make no discernible contribution to decision-making. They receive orders from the top which they have to carry out. This is the communist principle of "democratic centralism."

At the bottom of the power pyramid rests the Chinese public more than 96 percent of which are not Communist Party members. A few non-Party members are co-opted into state organizations but they have little voice. (See chapter 6.) Whoever turns against the Party or its policies becomes a class enemy, a counter-revolutionary and automatically, therefore, a criminal.

This system of all power to the Party is sanctioned by the concept of "dictatorship of the proletariat"--the Party being conceived as the vanguard of the proletariat. During the Maoist period, Mao went a step further. He tried to replace the Party with his personality cult and own Maoist organization which was introduced during the Great Proletarian Cultural Revolution (GPCR). The GPCR was launched in 1965 and in practice lasted until Mao's death in 1976; these were the so-called Eleven Calamitous Years.

Dengist Policies on Human Rights

While Mao's rule ended with his death, there is little evidence that decision-making power is not as centralized as it ever was. The leadership has not given up its own prerogatives. Deng Xiaoping, albeit not occupying all the top positions in the Party and government, wields political power via personal edict and continues to make personally important, and some not so important, decisions. Deng criticizes Mao's arbitrary rule, but as he makes progress in consolidating power, he has ruled in a personal way more and more. It is said, for example, that in 1979 he personally decided on the war with Vietnam and many of its operational aspects, that he had to give his personal blessing for publications of books, and had even to give his personal blessing for the marriage between a French student and a citizen of the People's Republic.[7] He even publicly repudiated his former Foreign Minister Hung Hua and former Defense Minister Geng Biao on their statements that the PLA would not be stationed in Hong Kong after 1997.[8]

Elections held under the Deng regime are no more free or representative than those held under Mao. Meetings of the Party Congress and its Central Committee have become more frequent but not more meaningful. More public use has been made of the National People's Congress to which a number of new members have been added, many also co-opted simultaneously into the Party; however, the Party Central Committee still is at best a sounding board for the leaders' new policies and the National People's Congress, perhaps a little more prestigious than before, remains largely a rubber stamp as long as control within the Party is not in serious factional dispute.[9] In some recent elections, two candidates have been nominated for a single position, but both were carefully selected with Party approval. Advancement within the Party depends upon loyalty, infighting ability, craftiness and access to the right faction. In short, though Mao's particular excesses have gone, the character of the communist system in China has not changed, not only in its institutional and doctrinal make-up, but also in the exercise of personal power and arbitrariness resulting from the concentration of power.

Deng has made an effort to reform the Chinese Communist Party by recruiting younger, better educated, and less hidebound Party members and by basing advancement more on merit than before, especially in economic matters. This, however, has little effect on China's human rights position. The Party, purged or not, still is the receptacle of all power and privilege. Mass drives or campaigns are still used to carry out specific policies against real or imagined dangers and enemies in an extra-legal way, as they were under Mao.[10] The individual, except for new economic freedoms that are intended to stimulate economic growth (see Chapter 5), is still relegated to a role of insignificance, while the nation's goals as determined by the Party crowd his or her rights out entirely.

In 1978 and 1979, when Deng was still fighting for control against Hua Guofeng and other opponents, there appeared some serious talk about new policies that included granting freedoms of speech, association, etc. But that was short-lived. When Deng's position became stronger, in an anti-crime drive targeted against political trouble-makers as well as common criminals, Deng showed his ruthlessness, demonstrating little regard for human rights on his part. Similarly, in an anti- "spiritual pollution" drive against greater freedom in art and literature as well as ideological deviation, he has frightened China's intellectuals who were just beginning to breathe a little freer.

It is sometimes argued that the communist one-party system is something less than a dictatorship because of the existence of factional divisions which in practice take the place of political parties. These factions, however, express power struggle at the top only and are not the equivalent of broad based political movements with grass-root support. In fact, totalitarian systems carry their struggles for power through factions and temporary alliances. The factions which existed under Mao,[11] as they do under Deng, have nothing to do with the exercise of political freedom. No communist faction has ever really gone to the people for a mandate. Deng only hinted at this in 1978-79. After his power was better consolidated, he has made no reference to any popular influence on choosing political leadership or to the exercise of rights by the people that may evolve toward this.

Wall Posters, "Free Speech" and "Democracy Wall"

The present status of the rights of free speech, petition and related political freedoms and the changes these rights have undergone can be traced to the early phase of the Cultural Revolution. At that time wall poster writing and demonstrations were organized by Mao and his faction to unseat his opposition. Big character posters and other forms of expression that were manipulated by Mao and his followers continued after the violent stage of the Cultural Revolution, with the exception of the period 1971-73 following the death of Lin Biao (who was accused of trying to assassinate Mao). Allowing expression of criticism of the regime was at that time considered too dangerous to political stability. However, wall posters as a form of protest were institutionalized again in 1973 with the "criticize Lin, criticize Confucius" movement, which was really targeted on Zhou Enlai.

In 1975 the right of putting up wall posters was guaranteed in the national constitution along with three other rights constituting the so-called "four big freedoms." The other three were "speaking out freely, airing views fully," and "holding great debates." These rights were also put into the 1978 constitution.[12] There was some belief, by optimists at least, that after Mao's death and with Deng in power, China might be heading in the direction of democracy of the Western type. Democracy Wall, where anyone could put up a "big character poster," flourished. Various complaints were also made against the government, in advocacy of political reforms and for the cause of human rights (or preventing human rights abuses). As it turned out, however, Deng, in much the same way as Mao, used the new "democratic" movement as a temporary tactic to weaken his opposition politically and to win public support for his struggle for power in the Party. After his victory at the Third Plenum of the Eleventh Central Committee in December 1978, Deng repudiated the Democracy Wall experiment--calling it "anarchistic, counter-revolutionary and reactionary."

A few months later the Democracy Wall was closed down. In early 1980 Deng went still further when he condemned the "four big freedoms" and publicly declared that they would be taken from the constitution. So the practice of free expression ended, constitutional provisions and solemn promises by Deng notwithstanding.[13]

After his seizure of power Deng appears to have faced opposition to his policies and competition for authority from factions in the Party organized against him. At the top levels of the Party, government and military, bureaucratic factions have engaged in various kinds of opposition to Deng's programs. But like factional struggles and factional problems in the past Deng's opposition has not gone to the people for a mandate. Neither has he.

To those who thought that the right of free speech, protest and other rights common to Western democracy really had a chance under Deng, their hope was dealt a sharp and perhaps fatal blow with the arrest and trial of dissident Wei Jingsheng. (See Chapter 4.) Wei's case was an example to all who believed that China was becoming a democracy or who thought that human rights and freedoms had blossomed in some real sense of the word. It also destroyed the view that the Communist Party was no longer an institution that could not be challenged with impunity and that it would allow individual rights above the Party and the state.

After the Wei case the trial of the Gang of Four and the anti-crime campaign further discouraged anyone who thought that the Communist Party and state had changed vis-a-vis basic freedoms and human rights. (See Chapter 4 for further details.) From this point on it was clear to the public in China that free speech and democracy, ostensibly rights under the constitution, were not real rights the individual could demand. The individual, it was clearly demonstrated, had no inherent rights vis-a-vis the state or the Party. To leaders like Deng "democracy" or "freedom" was a temporary slogan, a short-lived phenomenon. "Democracy" was also a facade to please Western countries that had become generous toward China and were essential for China for the "Four Modernizations" to succeed.[14]

Not only was the democracy and freedom of expression movement in China strangled during 1979-82 by the Wei case, the trial of the Gang, and the anti-crime drive, the campaign to eradicate "spiritual pollution" launched toward the end of 1983 portended broader and more far-reaching violations of human rights. For it brought back to millions of Chinese memories of the Cultural Revolution, reminding them that the promises made by the top leaders that the Cultural Revolution was over, never to happen again, might not be true.

Though the movement against "spiritual pollution" was used by Maoist radicals against what they contended were immoral influences caused by contacts with foreigners, especially Westerners, conservative elements in the Party supported it, apparently to preempt the Maoists and to prevent them from starting an anti-foreign and anti-rightist campaign. Leaders of the Dengist faction admitted that Western influence was making it more and more difficult for the Party to control the people and to justify the Party's special role in Chinese politics and its elite status. (See also Chapter 6.)

The anti-"spiritual pollution" movement assailed bright clothing, foreign music and art, dancing, pornography, women curling their hair and, among others things, persons raising goldfish. As the movement, like others in the past, got under way, individuals were attacked verbally and then brought in by local public security organs for questioning and even placed in jail or sent to re-education camps for consorting with foreigners (particularly foreign news reporters), playing foreign games (including sports--though this was, of course, selective), learning a foreign language, and much more. As the campaign entered a more frenzied stage, books in libraries and unversities were burned.

Philosophically, the movement attacked the notions that "alienation" (see Chapter 6) can occur in both capitalist and socialist nations and that Western-style humanism can have some application in socialist countries. If the latter were true, it would mean that individuals inherently deserve some human rights not officially granted by the Party or the regime.[15]

Compulsory Population Control

Though China clearly has a population problem, which in the minds of many both in China and in foreign countries justifies a program to limit population growth, the problem itself is in large part a creation of the "system" and of Mao's policy. Moreover, the harsh means of dealing with the problem by the Chinese Communist Party can hardly be justified by even the most sympathetic approach to the issue.

When the present government came to power in 1949, Mao declared that China had no population problem and that the notion of overpopulation was a "capitalist myth" created as a justification for oppressing the working class. Based on Marx's labor theory of value, Mao said that a person's hands (in a situation of equal distribution under socialism) could produce more food than his mouth could eat; therefore a population problem was impossible. Mao even hinted that China's huge population was an asset because it meant that if in a nuclear war China were to lose one half of its population, there would still be an ample population left to carry on in the aftermath which was portrayed as a magnificent socialist future.

Mao changed his position on population control in the mid-1950s after China's first census. However, when he launched the Great Leap Forward and the commune program a few years later, he dropped plans for meaningful population control before it could really get under way and returned to the theme that a large and rapidly expanding population was desirable. Just before the launching of the Great Leap, in 1957, Ma Yinchu, an economist of high repute and President of Peking University, dared to propose a birth control program. He was subsequently branded a rightist and was removed from his position. He remained in disgrace for the next twenty years.

After a few years official attitude again changed, but it reversed itself several times before the current policies on population control were established. Even as late as 1974 the Chinese government, in response to policies adopted at the Belgrade World Population Conference, condemned birth control as a "wicked imperialist plot" to hold down the populations of Third World nations and to perpetuate imperialist mastery of the developing world.[16]

Reversing Mao's policies, in 1978, and coinciding with the Four Modernizations slogan, Deng gave population control top priority. The Party explained that it was necessary in order for China to sustain economic growth. To ensure that the new policies were carried out, salary bonuses, privileges in educational benefits and housing were given to those that signed pledges to have only one child or those that had only one or two. When it was realized that this program was not working as well as had been hoped and that incentives to stimulate agricultural production were increasing the demand to have children, especially males, rewards and punishments became more extreme.

Severe discrimination in job assignments, housing and education was instituted. Women began to have their monthly cycles monitored by cadres or government officials. Maternity leaves were cancelled beyond the first child. Food and medical allotments were limited to only one or two children per family--thus depriving additional children of sustenance. Paychecks were cut for parents that had more than one child. Mandatory interviews were conducted regarding the use of birth control devices. Finally, conception required prior permission by the local cadre and women who became pregnant "illegally" were forced to undergo abortions-- even in late months of pregnancy. (See Chapter 5 for further details on this point.)

The psychological impact of China's one-child rule is bound to be tremendous on second and third children who somehow survive and later learn of the effect their births have had on their older brother or sister and parents. Older children would, of course, be made to resent or hate their younger siblings for the deprivation they have endured. The birth control program can also have social class effects. Children in one-child families have, or will, become a privileged class; second or third children are automatically outcasts, for reasons over which they have no control.[17]

China's birth control policies have also produced a multitude of horror stories. In the rural areas where farm families need a male child to help with the farm work later, girl children are often killed at birth. In many areas it has, in fact, become the custom to take a bucket of water to a delivery in order to drown the baby after it is born if it is female. In worse cases older girl children, sometimes even teenagers, are murdered so that the family can under Communist regulations legally have another child in an effort to get a boy.

There have also been widespread reports of "barefoot" doctors sterilizing people several times, tying urinary tubes when trying to give a vasectomy, nurses quitting their profession after hearing late period babies scream or seeing them grimace in pain as they are born following a lethal injection. Many mothers are reported to hide their pregnancy or have the baby in seclusion and try to feed it with inadequate food, then failing in this, committing infanticide or suicide or both.[18]

Clearly the human rights abuses associated with China's population control program are legend. Even far less draconian population control policies may have been a factor in the fall of Indira Ghandi's first administration. Will the Chinese people, at present apparently cowed, continue to tolerate indefinitely such inhuman treatment? Where will the present policy lead? Chinese scientists have recently taken an interest in approaches to eradicating hereditary diseases and many have advocated that China's birth control program, since one child is the limit, should insist on "no children" for people with "congenital" disease--including mental disorders or "criminal tendencies."[19] Who is to define criminal tendencies, or to predict them? The potential human rights abuses of these policies one can only imagine.

Freedom of Religion

In all of China's past constitutions religious freedom was guaranteed. It is promised in the constitution of 1982. Practice, however, was never as promised; it varied from period to period. The initial policy after the Communist seizure of power was one of persecution. In the years of the first political drives, many religious leaders, especially Westerners, were imprisoned and maltreated and large numbers lost their lives. Temples, churches and mosques were desecrated and used for secular purposes; religious services were suppressed. However, as a result of the great suffering during the Cultural Revolution adherence to a religious faith actually increased for many who observed religious services underground. Perhaps because of the government's inability to suppress religion totally and at the time when China began to turn to the West for economic and technical aid, official policy toward religion changed somewhat for the better in the late 1970s. There was an open resurgence of religious practice.

But since then there have been efforts to make sure that this does not go too far. Hardest hit has been Buddhism, particularly in Tibet. Tibetan priests have been executed and incarcerated in forced labor camps. Government persecution by force included the vast scale and systematic destruction of temples and monasteries, and wholesale burning and destruction of religious texts and artifacts, aimed apparently at the eradication of the faith and the whole Tibetan culture.

Islam, being more militant, has been able to protect itself better although atrocities have been committed against Muslims and Mullahs. During the Cultural Revolution, for instance, the Red Guards did not dare to attack mosques and Muslim communities in such cities as Sian or in the Uigur Autonomous Region of Central Asia for fear of open warfare.

Christianity was doubly odious for the Communists because of its Western connection. Both Protestant and Catholic churches have been reorganized as national Chinese churches, and Catholics are being prevented from having any contact with the Holy See. Bishops and archbishops who have refused to abandon Rome have been imprisoned or in many cases reimprisoned, sometimes for decades. Religious meetings are overseen carefully and are made to conflict with mandatory political activities. A new threat to religious tolerance came with the anti-"spiritual pollution" drive. Those who practice religions are automatically suspected of having foreign connections. While religious services and the erection of religious buildings have been allowed, in many cases there has been official discouragement or intimidation of those who exercise the right. This may be indicative of the fear of officials to commit their reputations and careers to granting religious rights in the event that the political lines change again.[20] However, a countervailing factor is the practical need of not over-straining the carefully nurtured Western connection. Political reality is the key. (See also Chapter 6.)

The Unemployed, the Aging and Women

Officially, the People's Republic of China has no unemployment. In fact, this is one of the advantages claimed for the communist system. For this reason statistics on unemployment do not exist. Government officials have, however, mentioned on occasion ten to twenty million young people in China's cities (where only about 15 percent of the population resides) "waiting for work." The official news agency, Xinhua, has also announced that 70.5 percent of all urban youths have jobs--implying that 29.5 percent do not.[21] Equally serious, or more serious than the problem of the unemployed (or "awaiting jobs"), is the large underemployment in both rural areas and in the cities.

Since the rural problem is less overt, the government simply enforces a policy of preventing people from moving to the cities. In other words, the unemployment problem is a cause for restricting freedom of travel and residence. It also lends itself to forms of discrimination or human rights violations inasmuch as opportunities for self-generated employment are blocked as are the freedoms which make such activity possible. The latter official position has changed somewhat for the better following Deng's "Four Modernizations" policy. (See Chapter 5.) However, due to the impact of the baby boom of the 1950s and 1960s, the size of the problem has increased and it is possible that restrictions on travel will again be tightened. The government also sees to it that political troublemakers are either incarcerated in labor camps or are unable to have employment outside.

In principle, the Chinese communist system advocates sex equality. All the constitutions, including that of 1982, proclaim the society's concern about women and children. In practice, families are often separated, sometimes for years. Mao's Marriage Law on the surface maintained equal rights of women in the marriage relationship although this had been accepted already in the earlier civil code under the

Nationalists. What the Communists wanted to stress, however, was the role of women as activists in their revolution.

The Communist Party's record on its promise of sex equality was poor; the figures are not impressive. Women comprise 24 percent of the membership of the Party but the percentage diminishes with increase in rank. Only one full member of the Politburo, the widow of Zou Enlai, is a woman. More important still, no member of the Party Secretariat is female; there is no woman in the top ranks of the military. In the provincial structure there are no woman Party first secretaries and no woman provincial governors.[22] Chen Muhua, an alternate member of the Politburo and counterpart of the U.S. Secretary of Commerce on the Joint U.S.-China Trade and Commercial Commission, has been publicly criticized for corruption in the Chinese media for actions that are commonplace in China. Besides, the central issue is their exclusion from real power. The one exception was Jiang Qing, Mao's widow, whose grasp for supreme power met with failure and who has become the butt of nationwide derision and ridicule.

The chance for a larger share in important positions in the future is dimmed by a continued discrimination of women in education. While at the primary level half of the students are female, the corresponding figure at the high school level is only 40 percent, and at the university level, 23 percent. On the other hand, eighty percent of China's illiterates are women while sixty to seventy percent of those "awaiting jobs" are said to be women.[23]

Women are now in the workplace--but this is often not by choice; they have to work to live and they are pushed into occupations that, outside farm work, carry low pay. Even in the jobs where women do work along with men, they are usually awarded fewer work points because they are physically weaker or because work points are given to the head of the household instead of the individual woman workers (in the case of farm work).

Because of the experience of Jiang Qing and the interest in getting the economy moving, which is assumed to be a male aptitude, women are not doing better in China now than they were five or ten years ago. It is increasingly evident to foreign observers taking the best forms of transportation and eating in the best restaurants that there are almost no female Chinese customers. Women increasingly complain of more wives being mistreated and abandoned; the gap in physical appearance between men and women in middle age and the hardship of divorce on women are readily observable and common knowledge.

Most of China's children are taken care of by working women or grandmothers. (Only slightly over one-fourth of the children are in day care centers.) This compares to over half of young children who are put in day care centers part of the time in the United States. Women live longer in China than men, but the discrepancy is less than in most other countries, especially Western nations. Finally, notwithstanding the recent increase in the availability of consumer goods, disposable diapers, washing machines, and all goods that make women's life easier are seen only infrequently in the People's Republic of China.

But perhaps the gravest injury to women's rights is the manner in which population control policies have been enforced.

Older people suffer in China--notwithstanding their venerated role in the pre-communist past when most people looked forward to a better life as they aged. In the first place, they suffer from job discrimination. With unemployment high, men (except Party members[24] and government employees) are forced to retire at age 60 or earlier. For women the retirement age is 50. A special privilege some older workers in public employment enjoy is the promise of a job for a child at the father's place of work if the latter retires early. What is even worse, due to widespread feelings of resentment, frustration and even hatred in the society where many are alienated from the system, older citizens suffer because of physical weakness. In the countryside especially when there is a shortage of food, they get less, while those who can work in the fields get more.[25] They have less access to public amenities in the cities. Although the government has provided stipends for some retirees and has built some living facilities for older citizens, the stipends are usually not sufficient and by the government's own admission, few houses for the aged are run well and funds to build them or keep them running are sorely inadequate.[26]

Elderly people are generally denied hospital care because of the lack of sufficient medical facilities. Thus, after they are in the hospital for a short time (if they are admitted) they are forced to go home. In fact, most deaths in China occur at home without medical care. Many elderly oppose cremation, but they have no choice; they cannot be given burials. In short, Confucianism in terms of respect and loving care for the elderly is no longer seen in the People's Republic of China.[27]

In all these matters the Chinese communist system not only asserts that it guarantees human rights but claims to have expanded their social significance. In practice though, actual policies often turn out to have quite contrary results. It is readily apparent that the nature of the Chinese polity is the ultimate cause of various human rights abuses. Some may try to justify the absence of human rights by noting that China's political system is not Western. However, many nations

around the world have good to excellent human rights
records and have not simply adopted Western democracy.
Moreover, in claiming such an explanation for China's
human rights failures, one is admitting that China's
communist system by its very nature discriminates
against the individual, especially in exercising human
rights.   Hence, if the situation is to improve, the
system itself must be changed. If this is unlikely to
happen, then it is unlikely that China's human rights
situation changed in any permanent way in the late 1970s
and early 1980s. We have provided much evidence and
logical argument that it has not. It is unlikely too
that the situation will change in any positive way in
the future of the Chinese Communist Party's own
volition.

ENDNOTES

1. For a definition of human rights, see also Jack C. Plano and Roy Olton, The International Relations Dictionary (Santa Barbara: ABC Olio Press, 1982), p. 316.

2. On the other hand, Chinese leaders have publicly assailed the Soviet Union for its human rights situation mentioning that the Soviet Union is "a land of KGB agents, with prisons of citizens with many others exiled." In these criticisms they imply that China's human rights record is better and in many cases have used Western standards of human rights to make this argument. Chinese officials have also publicly stated that the human rights record of the United States is better than the Soviet Union's--again contradicting their criticism of a "bourgeois democratic" standard of human rights. For further details on these statements and views, see Peking Review, March 11, 1977, pp. 23-24.

3. Mao Tse-tung, "On the People's Democratic Dictatorship," June 30, 1949, in Selected Works of Mao Tsetung, Vol. 4 (Peking: Foreign Languages Press, 1961), p. 418. Five percent of even the 1949 Chinese population (541 million according to Chungkuo T'ung chi Nien chien. (China Statistical Yearbook) (Hong Kong: Ching-chi tao-pao, 1983) (Hong Kong: Economic Bulletin Publishers), would be well over 25 million persons on the Chinese mainland.

4. See Franz Michael, Mao and the Perpetual Revolution (Woodbury, N.Y.: Barron's Educational Service, Inc. 1977).

5. Ibid.

6. See Derek J. Waller, The Government and Politics of Communist China (New York: Doubleday & Co., Inc., 1971).

7. Jay and Linda Mathews, One Billion: A China Chronicle (New York: Random House, 1983), p. 155.

8. Report by Frank Ching, The Wall Street Journal, June 27, 1984.

9. As head of the Standing Committee of the National People's Congress, Peng Chen has apparently gained

more power for it at perhaps the expense of the Party under the possibly closer control of Deng. But this may reflect more of a power struggle targeted at Deng by Peng who headed the early drives against counter-revolutionaries and played again a leading role in the anti-crime drive discussed below. See Fr. L. La Dany, "China's New Power Centre?" in Far Eastern Economic Review (Hong Kong), Vol. 121, June 28, 1984, pp. 38-39.

10. For a fuller account of these drives, see Mu Fu-sheng, The Wilting of the Hundred Flowers: The Chinese Intelligentsia under Mao (New York: Praeger Publishers, 1963); also, Mathews, One Billion, Section III; and Fox Butterfield, China: Alive in the Bitter Sea (New York: Bantam Books, 1983), pp. 364-365.

There were a multitude of such drives under Mao. Among the more notorious ones were the agrarian reform drive against landowners and richer peasants, the anti-counter-revolutionary drive, the three-anti drive against officialdom, the five-anti drive against businessmen, and the thought reform drive, all in the earlier years; the anti-rightist drive to destroy the opposition that was revealed in 1956-57, the Great Leap Forward of 1958-59, the Socialist Education movement of the early sixties, and, to top it all, the Great Proletarian Cultural Revolution.

11. Mao was opposed by several regional factions in the early and mid-1950s. In the late 1950s two major factions in the Party aligned against him to slow down his further pursuit of leftist policies like the Great Leap Forward and the organization of communes in China. For a while they were even powerful enough to force Mao to resign from his post as chief-of-state. Later, during the Cultural Revolution, the Liu Shaoqi faction was destroyed while Chou Enlai's faction was almost decimated. Lin Biao's faction was later eliminated after he was killed. The "Gang of Four" ruled China very briefly in the wake of Mao's death only to be overthrown by Hua Guofeng and other conspirators most of whom Deng has since purged. But none of this promoted either democracy or human rights.

12. Article 13 in the 1975 constitution and Article 45 in the 1978 constitution.

13. The 1982 constitution no longer contains the same provision on "big character posters," etc. See also David Bonivia, The Chinese: A Portrait (New

York: Penguin Books, 1980), p. 267.

14. Bonivia, The Chinese, pp. 274-275.

15. See New York Times, April 13, 1984.

16. See Richard Bernstein, From the Center of the Earth: The Search for the Truth about China (Boston: Little, Brown & Co., 1982).

17. Bonivia, The Chinese, p. 97.

18. See Stephen W. Mosher, Broken Earth (New York: Free Press, 1983).

19. Mathews, One Billion, p. 37.

20. See Bonivia, The Chinese, p. 72.

21. Butterfield, China, p. 190.

22. Butterfield, China, p. 168.

23. Ibid, p. 166.

24. Deng has pressured some older Party stalwarts (the so-called "Long March veterans" who went to Yenan in the 1930s) to retire but apparently only those not supporting him.

25. See James Kenneson, "China Stinks," Harpers, April 1982.

26. Du Ranzhi, "Old People in China: Hope and Problems," Beijing Review, April 16, 1984, p. 32.

27. Bonivia, The Chinese, p. 30.

4
The Legal Dimension

Introduction
    In the humanist, Western tradition human rights are
protected by law. While the concept of human rights is
of relatively recent origin in historical terms, their
protection by law dates from much earlier times. In
China, the legalist tradition, though taking a backseat
to the ethical rule of Confucianism, helped uphold the
social order throughout the imperial times up to our
century. (See Chapter 2.) Nor was Confucianism anti-
law per se. When the imperial era ended, the
Nationalists in their efforts to establish a unified
nation-state and a modern economy introduced a complete
system of Western codes and legal institutions. In
fact, rule by law worked relatively well during the
Nationalist period given the environment of war and
civil strife.
    When the Communists came to power, however, they
totally abolished the previous codes and institutions.
Under Mao, they went even further than their confreres
in the Soviet Union. They did not substitute "communist
law" for what had existed before. They introduced no
civil and criminal legal order, and instead ruled in an
arbitrary and essentially "lawless" way. This was part
of Mao's plan to increase the state's political control
over the individual and to create his ideal "socialist
man." The only new laws of any importance promulgated
after the establishment of the People's Republic dealt
with the structure of the political system.[1]
    In retrospect it is known that Mao Zedong refused
to be bound by any set rules, even of his own, and
preferred to impose his policies through political
drives and campaigns. He sought to govern by directives
which did not deal with acts of individuals, but instead
were aimed at groups in society targeted by his
policies. Enemy groups were often defined on a
percentage (of the population) basis, to be treated
according to varying degrees of harshness that were
preplanned. These campaigns could be turned on and off
as Mao saw fit or found necessary, which was a great

41

advantage to him.

Since the death of Mao in 1976, the Chinese communist leadership has introduced legal codes as it had tried to do twice before during the last decades, only to be frustrated by Mao.[2] In the communist conceptual framework, the purpose is, however, not to protect the freedom of the individual, but to use law as a tool of the dictatorship of the proletariat. In short, the goal is, or appears to be at this juncture, to establish communist law.

An important reason for wanting rules or laws on this occasion is to provide a semblance of a legal framework for dealing with salient social changes resulting from new economic goals. Another reason is to satisfy the needs of foreign businessmen for more precise rules in economic matters. This has led to the writing of a new criminal code of 1979 and to laws on economic dealings involving foreigners.

Leaving aside the regulations affecting foreigners, the People's Republic of China appears to be in the process of moving from a Maoist state of no laws to one of communist law. Under this framework the rights of individuals are secondary to the interests of the Party, the socialist program, the dictatorship of the proletariat and the Marxist-Leninist-Mao Zedong thought doctrine. This, as will be seen below, is the spirit behind the efforts to develop "constitutionalism."

China's Constitutions

It is noteworthy that when Mao seized power in 1949 he had no constitution which he could use as the basic framework for government or as the foundation of the nation's legal system. In fact, a constitution was not enacted for five years. During the first five years three documents served in place of a constitution: (1) The Organic Law of the Chinese People's Political Consultative Conference, (2) The Common Program of the Chinese People's Political Consultative Conference, and (3) The Organic Law of the Central People's Government. The first contained laws hastily passed by an anti-Kuomintang united front organization in September 1949. The second was an ideological treatise and policy statement defining class enemies and stating who should be "re-educated." It guaranteed equality of rights for women and minority groups in very vague terms; otherwise it stated who did not have rights rather than who did and what they were. The third was a set of laws mixed with a party platform which gave the power of interpretation of the laws to the Central People's Government Council--not the courts. The courts were simply an operational arm of the government. The government in turn was controlled by the top leadership of the Chinese Communist Party.

The reason for mentioning these early developments

is that they underscore certain aspects of the political system. The reasons that the PRC leadership refrained from writing a constitution are many and are important. First of all, it was assumed that a constitution would freeze the political status quo, that it would impede social development and that it might create a new ruling class.[3]

In short, a constitution would hamper the development of a totalitarian system because, if observed, it would regularize the exercise of power and limit it. A constitution was also considered anti-Marxist in that it implies something unchanging in human nature. According to Marx, in a class society there is no human nature as such, only class nature. Finally, constitutional guidelines assume that administrative processes and politics are separate and distinct and that power is associated with a post, not an individual. Mao wanted to rule China based upon his moral superiority (as seen by the success of the revolution) and sought to mold the Chinese nation under him.

In 1954 the People's Republic of China wrote its first constitution. It did so to give importance to bureaucratic institutions that were needed to rule the country rather than to establish the rule of law. Courts and a system of prosecution were delineated in this constitution—though both had to work with local congresses and were subordinate to the Party. Also this document included, or incorporated, much of the pre-1954 regulatory principles that were used in managing the country. In short, the system was not changed as a result of enacting a constitution. Certainly the cause of human rights and freedoms did not benefit. Moreover, from 1957 on, after the "rightists" had criticized the government for not codifying the law, the Party responded by launching an anti-rightist campaign, and the constitution was almost completely ignored. The prospects of its serving as a basis for a legal system practically ceased to exist.[4]

Another constitution was written in 1975. From the point of view of the eventual establishment of the rule of law it was regressive rather than progressive. Instead the constitution stressed the importance of the rule of the CCP, the dictatorship of the proletariat and Marxism-Leninism and the Thought of Mao Zedong. Prosecution and legal trials were linked to political processes and assumed mass participation. The lines of legal authority as specified in this constitution were blurred—apparently purposely so. In a sense, this constitution was a faithful reflection of the political attitude of the government then under Maoist control.

Just three years later, in 1978, and two years after Mao's death, a third constitution was enacted, this one containing provisions for guarantees of various rights for large segments of the population. It also made provision for a procuratorate--to oversee legal compliance by government bodies below the State Council level. In a number of other ways--on paper--it can be considered much better in terms of providing legal and human rights than the 1975 Constitution. It was longer and more specific. It departed from the political (and legal) thinking that went into the Cultural Revolution. On the other hand, it grew out of the post-Mao Hua Guofeng years and partly reflected Hua's thinking. It did not officially repudiate the doctrines of the Cultural Revolution and did not go very far in institutionalizing any legal system of restraints upon the Party or checks to other avenues of arbitrary power and authority.

In 1982 China's current constitution was debated and at the end of the year put into force. As a document upon which a legal system and the rule of law can be built it is superior to its two predecessors and in many ways resembles the 1954 constitution. It is more detailed in terms of the protections and rights it affords the individual and it gives more authority to the government as opposed to the Chinese Communist Party--making the National People's Congress (NPC) a seemingly autonomous law-making body.[5] It also provides a better foundation for a legal branch of government that might operate independently.

On the other hand, there are fundamental defects or limitations in this document if it is to become the basis for a system ruled by law. First, this constitution, like others before it, confirms the "dictatorship of the proletariat"--meaning the supremacy of the Chinese Communist Party. It does not exclude Party control over the legal process. In short, the government--and the courts--are as before subordinate to the Party. This being the case, there is no judicial independence and therefore no rule of law. If the Party decides to overrule the courts, it can. If it chooses to put political decisions or the goals of mass movements above the law, it can. Another reason for questioning this document is that the provisions mentioning the courts in the 1982 constitution are taken almost verbatim from the 1954 Constitution. Looking at what happened to the courts following the anti-rightist campaign in 1957, after which there was no legal education in China for more than two decades, there is justification for worry about the future of the legal system and the courts under the 1982 constitution.[6] Clearly nothing has been added that would make possible a trend towards a meaningful legal system based on the separation of powers and checks and balances.

Besides, basic individual rights are more restrained than in the 1978 Constitution. For example, the right to write and post big character posters is not mentioned in the 1982 Constitution. Nor does the new constitution protect the rights of correspondence and publication and, for workers, the right to strike--which were provided in the 1978 Constitution. Finally, basic democratic privileges are not discussed in detail or guaranteed to the degree they nominally were in the 1978 Constitution.7

One should also remember that the 1982 constitution, as all the earlier constitutions, was passed in the context of the writing of a new Chinese Communist Party constitution. The Party constitution gives no indication that the Communist Party is abandoning any of its prerogatives or is turning over legal authority to the state, or is in any way about to allow checks and balances to operate or to contemplate the idea of an independent judiciary. The timing, as well as other events and provisions, suggests that it is meant to be a document subordinate to the Party constitution just as the government and its legal branch are subordinate to the policies of the Party.

With the document of 1982, China has its fourth constitution in thirty-three years. If the 1949 documents are counted, it is the fifth, not counting the drafts of 1970 and perhaps of 1973. There might well be more. Hence it is doubtful that the provisions of the 1982 constitution have much permanence or can be thought of as binding in the sense that they will serve as restraints on the power of the Party, or the Party and the state in tandem. Party authorities can be expected simply to write another constitution as they see fit; clearly China's constitutions have provided no foundation on which to anchor a legal system or a guarantee of any other promise that affords serious, permanent protection of legal individual rights under the Communist Party. Instead its constitutions always play a propaganda role. They are a facade to impress the outsider with promises of rights and privileges for the individual.

China's Legal System

If Mao's rule was arbitrary, the question remains whether the reforms introduced after Mao's death can become the basis for an improved legal order.

During the Mao period China's political system was generally undifferentiated, i.e., it did not have a division of power between the making of law, law enforcement and adjudication. The police and the Party did all three. There was little concern with procedures or with violations of individuals' rights. The seriousness of a crime and the punishment depended on the "counter-revolutionary" implications and the class status of the person committing the crime. Peasants were usually not punished as severely for the same crime as were landlords and other social classes while those in power were often exempt from the law.8

The guilt or innocence of the accused was usually established during a pre-trial investigation but once arrested, a person's claim of innocence would only aggravate his punishment. (See Appendix) Actual trials were often for public show, to intimidate the population with the consequences of opposing the Party's authority. The accused was not provided with legal defense. In addition to criminal prosecution the Chinese Communist Party provided an informal mediation role to handle civil cases. The Party "qualified" for such a role on the assumption that all violations of the law had political implications on which the Party was the sole authority. Punishment for serious crimes was execution. For other crimes it was usually "reform" or "re-education through labor." This was said to be both punishment and a means of reform. Most frequently, however, neither the terms nor the length of such punishment was specified.

In 1979, three years after Mao's death and one year after the writing of a new state constitution, new laws were written and put into effect. The Organic Law for People's Procuratorates and the Organic Law for People's Courts defined the structure of the procuratorates newly instituted under the 1978 constitution. The People's Republic of China's first true set of criminal codes containing 192 separate articles and regulations on criminal procedure of 164 articles went into force. They provided an unprecedented amount of specificity in judicial procedure and punishment. At the same time civil laws on joint ventures were also enacted.

The People's Republic of China also enacted an Arrest and Detention Act and a Provisional Act on Lawyers and took other steps in establishing a criminal justice system and a system assuming rule by law. By 1981 there were 6,800 lawyers in China of whom all but 500 were employed full-time. Law departments in the universities began to reopen and army officers began to receive judicial training. A mass legal education campaign was launched and legal research was encouraged by the government, including the publication of several law journals.[9]

There are several alternative explanations for this complete reversal of Party policy. The most common explanation is that Deng wanted to support the economic changes he introduced through institutional rule that would survive him. He may also have sought the approval of Western countries to gain their support for his economic programs. The introduction of legal procedures would also be needed in the elimination of what was left of Maoism after the death of Mao and to fill the vacuum of authority left by the fall of the authority figure. With a kind of new legislation China was in practice following in the footsteps of the Soviet Union by creating a "socialist legality" though the new regime would hardly be willing to admit this.

Assessing China's Legal System

Three subsequent events--the trial of Wei Jingsheng, the trial of the "Gang of Four," and the crackdown on crime using public executions give some indication how this system would be applied and how far it would protect individual and human rights.

Wei Jingsheng was a young man, who in 1978 and 1979 was at the forefront of the democracy movement--writing a journal advocating democracy as the "fifth modernization" and associating with foreigners to debate the subject and get ideas for his writings. Among other points Wei argued that many Chinese had become Nobel Prize winners outside of China, but not in China because democracy existed abroad but not at home. With his extensive and often highly sophisticated arguments Wei received much attention from both Chinese and foreigners. Because of his fame, he was regarded as a leader of the democratic movement--and the most important victim when the government acted to end it.

Wei was arrested in March 1979 and put on trial in October--for one day. Wei's friends and all foreigners were barred from the courtroom. An official indictment against Wei was never published. A provision of the Organic Law written in 1950 was cited against Wei, placing him in the category of "counter-revolutionary" because of his essays in the magazine Tan-Suo (Exploration). He was also charged with violating Article 1 of the constitution that speaks of the "dictatorship of the proletariat" and Article 56 which calls upon citizens to support the leadership of the Chinese Communist Party. In addition, Wei was accused of passing military secrets to foreigners about the Sino-Vietnamese War.

Wei was not permitted to have the counsel of his choice. In his own defense, Wei charged that there had been confusion in the judicial system before the new penal codes were enacted in 1979. He claimed that the term "counter-revolutionary" was completely vague and that under Article 45 of the 1978 constitution he had the right to freedoms of speech, correspondence, assembly, publication, association, parade, demonstration and strike, as well as the freedom to air views freely, write big character posters and hold great debates. Further he said that he had not had access to classified documents while in the military and could not be justifiably accused of giving away "secrets" that were in fact only hearsay.[10]

The court was not swayed by Wei's cogent defense and sentenced him to fifteen years of hard labor. The Supreme People's Court subsequently upheld the sentence. The fact that the New China News Agency reported the results of the trial immediately within less time than would have been required to translate the documents suggests that the trial had been rehearsed and that the decision about Wei's guilt had been reached before the trial.

Subsequently another writer, Liu Qing, was arrested for distributing copies of Wei's defense. He was given three years of "administration detention"--which meant hard labor in Shaanxi (Shensi) Province under the "education through labor" system. A man in Zhengzhou was reportedly later sentenced to eight years in prison for writing a "big character poster" defending Wei.[11]

The Wei case was a warning to other dissidents that the democracy movement had ended. It also showed that the new legal procedures did not guarantee the accused any basic rights. Equally impotent in this regard was the constitution. Moreover, such vague terms as "counter-revolutionary" were still going to be used against those who opposed the Party leadership. On the other hand, some saw a modicum of progress in the Wei trial arguing that the trial might not have been held had Mao been alive and rather than receiving a fifteen year prison sentence Wei would probably have been executed. In short, things could have been worse, and therefore they were better.

The second case to test China's new laws and to determine the course of this socialist legal system was the trial of the "Gang of Four." This trial, actually of ten defendants--the "Gang of Four" plus six members of the "Lin Biao clique"--began on November 20, 1980 lasting until January of 1981 for a total of 27 working days.[27]

The trial was held in secret though segments of it were televised after each day's session. In May secret pre-trial hearings had been held--reportedly with video tapes made for the Politburo to see before deciding whether to go ahead with the trial in secret or to show at least parts of it to the public.[13] The Chief Justice of China's Supreme Court presided over a quorum of 34 judges, seven of whom had no legal training whatsoever. Eight hundred and eighty persons attended but among them were no foreigners.

The 20,000 word indictment accused both groups of defendants of framing and persecuting state and Party leaders in order to overthrow the dictatorship of the proletariat and of killing and torturing people--listing 34,375 people as victims. The "Gang" was in addition charged with plotting an armed uprising in Shanghai after Mao's death. Members of the Lin Biao group were further accused of plotting Mao's assassination and attempting to stage an armed counter-revolutionary coup.[14]

All six of the Lin Biao Group pled guilty and presented no defense. Two of the members of the "Gang" also pled guilty and testified as witnesses against the other two. The key Maoist Chang Ch'un-ch'iao (Zhang Chunqiao)[15] however, sat in silence, apparently trying to demonstrate that the trial was staged and that any defense was useless. Jiang Qing, Mao's widow, argued with the court and the prosecution at every turn with defiance and contempt. She took the position that she had acted only in Mao's behalf and for the Central Committee and that if she were guilty they were also. She praised the accomplishments of the Cultural Revolution, noting whenever she could how many people participated and how Mao personally had launched the movement. She used every opportunity to glorify leftism and to criticize the present rightist leadership.

The two defendants who did not show humility and repentance were sentenced to death with a two-year reprieve. The suspension has been renewed, apparently already more than once. The others received sentences from 16 years to life.

In terms of fairness and due process the trial was a sham.[16] The accused had been under arrest for several years before they were charged. (The "Gang of Four" had already been in jail for over four years at the time of the trial; the others had been under arrest for nine years.) Defense lawyers raised no objections to any question during the trial, nor did they cross-examine any witness. They only asked for leniency. Private telephone conversations taped years earlier were allowed in the court as evidence.[17] Confessions which, according to the 1979 Legal Code could not be used to incriminate the accused, were rewarded and lighter sentences were imposed on those who made them.

In view of the violation of the rights of the accused, lack of due process and lapses in legal procedures one has to ask why segments of the trial were shown on TV for foreigners to watch and comment on. Deng may have perceived that simply by having a trial he might send the message that China had become a society of law and order--inasmuch as under Mao those charged would simply have been killed or imprisoned or would have become non-persons without a trial. Moreover, the Western press had treated Deng very well, in fact, with great kindness, and had made little or no criticism of China's legal system or its human rights record. Thus Deng may have been led to believe that he would again receive favorable publicity in the West.

Clearly Deng had political motives in holding the trial and publicizing it. He wanted to undermine Hua Guofeng's position, and succeeded. Testimony at the trial proved Hua's complicity with the "Gang," and his approval of death sentences and other similar acts during the period immediately after Mao's death when his authority was generally unchallenged. In fact, shortly after the trial Hua submitted his resignation from the premiership. Deng also wanted to undermine Mao's reputation and disgrace the radical leftists of the Mao era. However, he did not want to condemn Mao directly—since Mao still had many supporters and repudiating Mao would have been exploited by Soviet propaganda and be to Deng's disadvantage.

The charges made in the indictment included the accusation that the defendants damaged the dictatorship of the proletariat and committed counter-revolutionary acts, two charges often leveled against enemies of the state during the Maoist period. The use of these terms linked the trials to the system of the past. Yet Deng seemed to feel that a trial of any kind would be acclaimed as progress in both the West and China. For the removal of the "Gang" and the remnants of the Lin Biao Group was in itself proof of change and to Deng's political advantage in China.

In August 1983, following months of Party concern over an increase in crime (and reportedly immediately following an attempt on Deng Xiaoping's life by a group of ruffians), the government adopted a number of measures to change China's criminal laws and reduce the crime rate.[18] Five resolutions were passed at a Standing Committee meeting of the National People's Congress to deal with the crime problem: (1) a resolution on revision of the Organic Law of the Courts, (2) a resolution on the exercise by State Security Organs of the Public Security Organs' Power to Investigate, Detain, Hold Preliminary Hearings and Assist in Making Arrests, (3) a resolution on Procedures for Rapid Trial of Criminal Elements that Seriously Jeopardize Public Security, and (4) a resolution on Severe Punishment for Criminal Elements that Seriously Jeopardize Public Security.

The third resolution formalizes the power of the Ministry of State Security established just two months before with little fanfare. In fact, the new ministry appears to have the same powers as the KGB in the Soviet Union and may become a similar organ of repression. The fourth resolution permits speedy trials and relieves policy and judicial authorities of the requirements of protecting individual rights under the 1979 criminal code. The fifth resolution allows stiffer penalties than are allocated under the present legal code, making legal the widespread use of capital punishment.

The passing of these laws was followed by a campaign against crime in China whereby criminals were apprehended quickly and in large numbers, were put on trial (often in large numbers) and punished severely for their crimes—usually with long sentences in re-education camps or by execution. According to pronouncements of the Standing Committee of the National People's Congress the new codes would not be used to deal with economic or political crimes.[19] But they were. After all, disruption of social peace and public security is vague enough, and economic crimes were among the most serious and troublesome for the regime. According to local officials in Peking there had been over nine thousand cases of profiteering and over three thousand cases of smuggling in the city alone.[20] And just before the resolutions were passed China's official news agency had reported on the "still growing" problem of economic crimes.[21]

Within weeks foreign reporters were learning of public executions all over China (though they were not allowed to witness any of them). Posters were displayed in public showing the names of the accused. Later a red mark was made on the poster indicating they had been executed with a bullet in the back of the head from point blank range. This happened all over the country even though, according to the law, executions were not to be made public affairs. Actually, some executions were even televised. Moreover, in almost all cases there was little attention to the rights of the accused or to due process. The concern was with reducing the crime rate, which, according to many high Chinese officials, had increased because of the leniency of the law. According to others, it was caused by Deng's modernization program and contacts with "decadent capitalist" states.[22] In any case, Chinese leaders, perhaps based on the order originating from Deng, perceived that something had to be done quickly and that the rule of law (if such was indeed developing) could be sacrificed as could progress in human rights.

In October 1983 Amnesty International reported that 600 had been executed in China in the previous two months and that cases of torture had been reported. Amnesty appealed to President Li of the People's Republic of China, but with no results. Amnesty International Report 1983 subsequently cited its four main concerns about China: trials of political prisoners that fell short of internationally established standards, imprisonment of prisoners of conscience, detention without trial of political prisoners and use of the death penalty.[23]

By spring foreign reporters estimated that 5,000 people had been executed; the U.S. State Department put the number at between 3,000 and 5,000--most of them being put to death without legal procedures being observed or individual rights protected.[24] According to other sources the number was much higher.[25] The number of people who were "deported" to other parts of the country or punished through essentially administrative means (education through labor) was reportedly very high.

Coinciding with the crime suppression campaign was a political purge, and the two cannot be separated. A sizeable number of Party and government officials were arrested and some of them executed for crimes during this time. Since the rules of due process were not followed there is no way of knowing how many were accused and punished for criminal acts and how many for political reasons. (See Appendix.) It is possible that personal grievances were occasionally the basis of accusations, resulting in executions for various crimes. The wave of executions served to intimidate those who might defy the Party's policies.

The crime suppression movement also influenced free speech and the press. During the last half of 1983 and during early 1984 the spokesmen for free speech and free press were noticeably subdued. The same suppression happened to freedom of association and assembly.[26]

Conclusions

As these cases show, it is questionable whether the People's Republic of China has made any permanent progress in rule by law through the adoption of a new criminal code in 1979. As of 1984 there was little confidence among the people in the new laws of 1979. In understanding the public reaction it must be recalled that similar previous efforts toward rule by law had been abortive. It should be pointed out that the three issue areas just mentioned are not the only cases where due process has been ignored or flaunted. In 1982 it was reported in the Chinese press that there were still 4,237 political prisoners that were former members of the Kuomintang--apparently most or all still defined as criminals for acts committed prior to 1949. Meanwhile the government announced restrictions on lawyers working except under supervision and control of the "Lawyer Consulting Bureau." Attorneys never became defenders of the accused working for the latter, they are public servants working for the state who make sure that laws are properly applied.

As noted in the Appendix, a large number of dissidents are known to have opposed the government's actions in violation of the legal code of 1979. Unlike Wei Jingsheng nearly all of them have not been heard from again. They were not put on trial; they simply disappeared. Statistical evidence gathered on crimes in China suggests another interesting fact: the more serious the crime, the quicker it is dealt with in terms of procedural time. To protect human rights more serious crimes should on the average be granted more time for preparation to go to trial and in court. Finally, in general, Party members are let off more easily for the same offense than non-Party members, that is, if they are arrested in the first place. All persons are not equal before the law.

It appears likely that in the majority of future cases, Chinese officials will find sufficient excuses for dealing with ordinary political crimes, or just opposition to the Party, by other than official legal means. The reinstitution of a 1957 regulation on "education or rehabilitation through labor" in 1979 almost immediately after the new law codes were enacted certainly provides an alternative to proper criminal procedures. The 1983 resolutions give further justification for using extra-legal means to punish criminals--not to mention political enemies, counter-revolutionaries, dissidents, etc. The case of Wei Jingsheng, the trial of the "Gang of Four," and the crime suppression campaign of 1983-84 have intimidated most citizens who might want to resort to argument about legal procedures.

Assuming that China will need a working legal system for its economic modernization program the laws of 1979, applied or not, will not suffice. One may wonder where the trend will lead. If it follows the Soviet model, the law will be used as a means of coercion and intimidation. If China goes the Western route, it will have to revamp its political system in some serious ways. In fact, it could be argued that it will require nothing less than a revolutionary change to have working democratic ways. There is to date no real evidence that this is the direction in which China is going or that its leaders want to go. On the contrary, there is evidence, including the cases cited above and the anti-crime campaign, that China will use whatever law only for convenience and within the present political framework although China probably will not return to Maoism for reasons of economic development plans and contacts with the West. Where China is going in terms of a legal system is very uncertain. The trends as of 1984 do not favor or argue for rule by law.

ENDNOTES

1. The only exception to the lack of codification was the Marriage Law of 1950, which was, however, carried through in the form of a drive linked to the land reform campaign. This law replaced a more elaborate formal statute which had been a part of the Family Law promulgated by the National Government.

2. The first time was at the end of the initial drives in the mid-fifties. The second time came when Khrushchev started his de-Stalinization.

3. Peter R. Moody, Jr., *Chinese Politics After Mao: Development and Liberalization, 1976-1983* (New York: Praeger Publishers, 1983), p. 75.

4. For details on China's constitutions before the 1982 constitution, see Frederic M. Kaplan, Julian M. Sobin and Stephen Andors, *Encyclopedia of China Today* (Fair Lawn, N.J.: Eurasia Press, 1979(, Part II, Chapters 4 and 5.

5. On apparent efforts on the part of Peng Chen, one of the first victims of the Cultural Revolution, to strengthen the Standing Committee of the NPC at the expense of the Communist Party and the government dominated by Dengists, see L. La Dany, "China's New Power Centre?" *Far Eastern Economic Review* (Hong Kong), Vol. 121, June 28, 1984, pp. 38-39.

6. See "What's New in the New Constitution," *Ming Pao* (Hong Kong), June 1982 and "A Critique of the '1982 Constitution,'" *Pai Shing* (Hong Kong), May 16, 1982.

7. An interesting discussion of the 1982 Constitution relating it to China's legal system and comparing it to previous constitutions was presented by Constance A. Johnson at the annual meeting of the Association of Asian Studies in Washington, D.C. in May 1984.

8. For further details, see Herbert Han-pao Ma, "A Socialist Legal System for Communist China: Some Critical Thoughts," in Wei-ping Tsai (ed.), *Struggling for Change in Mainland China: Challenges and Implications* (Taipei: Institute of International Relations, 1980).

9. See Hungdah Chiu, "Chinese Law and Justice: Trends over Three Decades," Occasional Paper/Reprints Series in Contemporary Asian Studies, Number 7, 1982, pp. 19-22.

10. David Bonavia, The Chinese (New York: Pelican Books, 1982), p. 276.

11. Ibid, p. 274.

12. For background details, see Immanuel C. Y. Hsu, China Without Mao: The Search for a New Order (Oxford: Oxford Un. Press, 1982), pp. 126-140.

13. Butterfield, China, p. 357.

14. Hsu, China Without Mao, p. 129.

15. In the official English version of the report by Chang (Zhang) on the 1975 constitution (China Reconstructs, March 1975), his name was still rendered according to the Wade-Giles system of transliteration. The reader should note that Chang and Zhang refer to the same person.

16. No attempt was made to link policies to actual transmission of orders, executions and torture, though in general there could be little question about the responsibility of the defendants.

17. Butterfield, China, p. 358.

18. "China: New Purges," Time, October 31, 1983, p. 50.

19. New China News Agency, September 2, 1983.

20. Asiaweek, June 11, 1982.

21. New China News Agency, July 26, 1983.

22. The Official version was that the crime wave was caused by the previous ten years of turmoil lasting from 1966 to 1976 and the "Gang of Four."

23. Amnesty International Report 1983 (London: Amnesty International Publications), 1983, p. 91.

24. Country Reports on Human Rights Practices for 1983. (Report submitted to the Committee on Foreign Affairs, U.S. House of Representatives and the Committee on Foreign Relations, U.S. Senate by the Department of State), (Washington: U.S. Government Printing Office, 1984), p. 743.

25. Amnesty International (London), in its 1984 report on China, has elaborated further on this topic. An underground radio broadcast from China called SPARK reported that the number killed may be as high as one million. Obviously this was anti-government propaganda. Yet SPARK also reported on some specific cases that were subsequently reported in the official media in China.

26. Country Reports on Human Rights Practices for 1983, p. 747.

5
Human Rights
and Economic Realities

The individual who cannot by his or her own devices keep body and soul together is not in a good position to insist on political rights or to safeguard personal dignity and integrity. A government that is determined to control its subjects totally will wish to have complete power over the means by which they physically survive, not to say make a decent living. Hence the freedom to make conomic decisions and to pursue economic activities is an integral part of all other freedoms of the individual person. Economic freedom or lack thereof, therefore, has a central place in any evaluation of human rights in post-Mao China.

Economic Rights in Human Rights Declarations

The individual's "unalienable rights" to "life, liberty and the pursuit of happiness" in the American Declaration of Independence have clear economic implications. One of these is free choice of employment. Subsumed under that are the rights to refuse particular types of work, to move around freely looking for new work, and to ask for better terms. Implied too is the freedom to be self-employed or to become an entrepreneur and employer of others. Free choice in education and training, often a preparatory step to employment, must also be included. The free exercise of the individual's rights in these respects in 1776 presupposed private ownership of means of production though the right to property in general was not explicitly recognized until later.

Government intervention in a market economy has always been with us. Basically, however, such intervention differs from socialist, centralist planning because it does not question the three pillars of the market system: free market prices, the individual's freedom of choice in making economic decisions, and private ownership of property for the purpose of production.

The Great Depression of the thirties and the post-World War II preoccupation in the West with employment

levels increased government activities in the private
economy. Although economists are by no means unanimous
on the effectiveness of government action in reducing
unemployment and maintaining stability, governments of
all persuasions have in general attempted to deal with
both. In view of this historical situation,
international human rights pronouncements after World
War II have as a rule included provisions dealing not
only with the individual's economic freedom but also the
level of overall economic activity.

The United Nations Universal Declaration of Human
Rights of December 1948 contained economic provisions[1]
dealing respectively with:

(1) "the right to work, to free choice of
employment, to just and favorable conditions of
work and to protection against unemployment"
(Article 23);

(2) "the right to rest and leisure" _for everyone_
(Article 24), that is, not just certain
segments of the population;

(3) "the right to a standard of living adequate for
... health and well-being ... and the right to
security in the event of unemployment,
sickness, disability, widowhood, old age ..."
(Article 25);

(4) "the right to education" (Article 26).

The rights listed under (1) are precisely those implied
in the Declaration of Independence. Additionally, Article 17 states: "1. Everyone has the right to own
property along as well as in association with others.
2. No one shall be arbitrarily deprived of his
property." The provision clearly includes both individ-
ually owned private property _of all kinds_ (not just
property for personal use) and property owned by more
than one person (e.g., partnerships, corporations, and
cooperatives). Finally, Article 25 contains a statement
which concerns the role of women in economic and other
activities and is of special interest in the case of the
People's Republic of China: "Motherhood and childhood
are entitled to special care and assistance."

The December 1966 International Covenant on Economic, Social and Cultural Rights[2] reaffirms the 1948
Declaration but expands on certain points of particular
significance to the discussion at hand:

Free choice of work. First, the right to work
refers to that which a person "freely chooses or ac-
cepts." Furthermore, full and productive employment is
to be achieved "under conditions safeguarding fundamental political and economic freedoms to the individ-

ual." (Underline added, Article 6.)

Restrictions of the exercise of rights must be limited. Second, "the State may subject such rights only to such limitations as are determined by law only insofar as this may be compatible with the nature of these rights and solely for the purpose of promoting the general welfare in a democratic society." (Article 4) This is reinforced in Article 5.

Non-discrimination. Third, the Covenant stipulates that states are to guarantee that the rights "will be exercised without discrimination of any kind as to race, color, sex, language, religion, political or other opinion, national or social origin, property, birth or other status." (Italics added)

The special status of motherhood. Fourth, according to Article 10, "Special protection should be accorded to mothers during a reasonable period before and after childbirth." This is supplemented by Article 12 which advocates measures for reducing stillbirths and infant mortality.

Promises in PRC Constitutions Affecting Economic Rights

The PRC has borrowed much from the language of these generally accepted international concepts. Yet in doing so it has made radical alterations both in the text and in the actual conditions for the exercise of these rights. In most cases the rights have been negated. Furthermore, concepts and practices are introduced that are totally contrary to the original notion of free choice and of safeguards against abuse. The following are some of the provisions that have evolved in the post-Mao period.

In the 1975 PRC constitution promulgated on January 17 of that year or 18 months before Mao's death, relatively little of economic significance except the following was stated in the chapter on "The Fundamental Rights and Duties of Citizens."[3] Article 26 made it both a "right" and a duty of Chinese citizens "to support the socialist system." Article 27 mentioned the rights to work, education, and material assistance for old age, sickness and disablement, the same as in the UN documents. As one of its obligations, under the same article, the state also undertook to "protect marriage, the family, and the mother and child," a statement which will become more meaningful later in this chapter. The "freedom to strike" was listed in Article 28 along with other political rights citizens of the People's Republic supposedly should enjoy. In the introductory chapter, dealing with "General Principles," Article 9 offered the state's protection to "the citizens' right of ownership to their income from work, their savings, their houses, and other means of livelihood." Finally, Article 5 in the same chapter mentioned the existence of "mainly two kinds of ownership of the means of production:

Socialist ownership by the whole people and socialist collective ownership by working people." In the same article, workers not engaged in agriculture were said to be allowed "to engage in individual labor" provided that he did not "exploit" (read hire) others and provided that this activity would be within legal limits and undertaken with the agreement of urban neighborhood organizations or that of producton teams in rural communes." Aside from the last point, there was no mention of any freedom of individual enterprise in the 1975 constitution. Nor was there any reference to the individual's freedom of choosing the nature and place of work or of choosing the kind of education preparatory to such employment, the implied rights one usually finds in free market economies. These details deserve close attention on two counts.

First, the provisions of the 1975 constitution, which was presented to the Fourth National People's Congress on January 13, 1975, by Zhang Chunqiao, a leading defendant in the 1980 Gang of Four show trial, corresponded closely to a draft[4] approved on September 6, 1970 by the Second Plenum of the Ninth CCP Central Committee. The languages of the relevant articles in the two documents were often identical. This is not too surprising inasmuch as the Maoist radicals who were in control in 1975 were also dominant in 1970 although Lin Biao was still one of the top leaders. (Lin's physical elimination on Mao's orders took place not long afterwards.)

The second reason for starting with the 1975 constitution is the continuity and change one detects by comparing the first post-Mao constitution, adopted on March 5, 1978 at the first session of the Fifth National People's Congress, with the 1975 document. The 1978 document[5] kept much of the 1975 philosophy pertaining to rights and duties while changes of two kinds were made: promises of gradual improvement in the citizens' lives were coupled with unmistakable statements of pure Maoist vintage. Article 48 and 51 mentioned respectively the citizens' rights to work and education while Articles 49 and 50 affirmed the working people's rights to rest and material assistance in times of need. Furthermore, in Article 53 of the 1978 constitution, protection by the state of "marriage, the family, and the mother and child" was reiterated in the same language as in Article 27 of the 1975 document. Finally, Article 56 of the 1978 constitution, like Article 26 in 1975, made support of the socialist system an obligation of all Chinese citizens. "The state safeguards the socialist system," according to Article 18, "suppresses all treasonable and counter-revolutionary activities, punishes all traitors and counter-revolutionaries, and punishes new-born bourgeois elements and other bad elements." (Underline added.) This was a restatement of the content of Article

14 in the 1975 constitution.

Special points and amendments in the 1978 constitution were by no means less Maoist than in Zhang Chunqiao's time. A few quotations of economic import will be illustrative:

(a) "... We must oppose revisionism and prevent the restoration of capitalism. ..." (Preamble)

(b) "... Education must serve proletarian politics ... and must enable everyone ... to ... become a worker with both socialist consciousness and culture." (Article 13)

(c) "... A production brigade may become the basic accounting unit when its conditions are ripe." (Article 7) In 1975, the corresponding Article 7 stipulated that the production team, the lowest level unit in the commune organization, would be the basic accounting unit, which was indicative of greater decentralization while the production brigade is a larger unit that can have several teams under it.

Lastly, a significant addition in 1978, soon to be expanded, states that "the state advocates and encourages family planning." (Article 53)

Individual Rights and the Economic System in the 1982 Constitution

The second post-Mao and still current (Summer 1984) constitution was adopted on December 4, 1982, during the fifth session of the Fifth National People's Congress.[6] The same Congress had, at its first session, adopted the rather Maoist document of 1978. Through the years, the appearance of every new constitution was accompanied by an increase in its length, from 30 articles in 1975 to 60 in 1978 and 138 in 1982. The lengthiness of the latest constitution is partly the result of its greater comprehensiveness and the detailed descriptions it contains. In many respects, however, the 1982 constitution is really more in the nature of a detailed policy statement, and a listing of desirable goals as of a given time, than a set of lasting constitutional principles.

The PRC's adherence to socialism as a way of economic life is stressed in at least four places. "The socialist system," states Article 1 of Chapter One, "is the basic system of the People's Republic of China." "Sabotage of the ... system," therefore, "... is prohibited." As in 1975 and again in 1978, "socialist public ownership of the means of production ... (consists of) ownership by the whole people and collective ownership by the working people." (Article 6) In defense of the collectivist ideals underlying the system the state will not stop at half measures. In education, for instance, the state "combats capitalist, feudalist and other decadent ideas." (Article 24) But more effective means are provided in Article 28, for:

"The state maintains public order and suppresses treasonable and other counter-revolutionary activities; it penalizes actions that ... disrupt the socialist economy and other criminal activities, and punishes and reforms criminals."

Second, more individual enterprise is now permitted than in 1975 and 1978 but there are definitely limits, which are moreover changed from time to time. These potentially highly "revisionist" provisions are introduced with strict safeguards in Articles 8, 11, 13, and 15. "Working people who are members of rural economic collectives have the right, within the limits prescribed by law (underline added) to farm private plots of cropland and hilly land, engage in household sideline production and raise privately owned livestock." Article 11 concedes that the "individual economy" or urban and rural workers, operating within the legal limits, should be "a complement (not an equal partner) to the socialist public economy." Under the same article, the state promises to protect the legitimate rights and interests of the individual economy but will also guide, supervise, and administratively control it. Article 13 expands the citizen's right to earned income, personal savings and ownership of residential housing and "other lawful property" ("other means of livelihood" in Article 9 of the 1978 constitution) to the "right to inherit private property." However, Article 15 erects once more a socialist safeguard by reaffirming the practice of "economic planning on the basis of socialist public ownership" and "the supplementary role of regulation (of the economy) by the market." Unmistakably and emphastically, states Article 15:

> Disturbance of the orderly functioning
> of the social economy or disruption of
> the state economic plan by any organi-
> zation or individual is prohibited.

The means of enforcement of the prohibition has already been stated in the last paragraph. It also finds support in Chapter 3[7] of the 1979 Criminal Code.

In the third place, like its predecessors, the 1982 constitution mentions the citizens' rights to work (Article 42), to rest (Article 43, for working people only), to material assistance (Article 45), and to education, which is also a duty (Article 46). Article 49 repeats the frequently promised protection of "marriage, family, and mother and child." In general, the 1982 constitution is more explicit than the 1978 document in stating what the drafters believed the state should do in many areas; the statements resemble political campaign promises of better things to come.

Two issues of importance to the discussion below

should be stressed, however: First, Article 25 states, "The state promotes family planning so that population growth may fit the plans for economic and social development." Article 49 adds, "Both husband and wife have the duty to practice family planning." The second issue concerns the citizen's right to work and the need for expanding employment opportunities. In this connection, while Article 42 reaffirms the right <u>and</u> duty to work, it also expands the promise:

> Using various channels, the state creates conditions for employment, strengthens labor protection, improves working conditions, and, on the basis of expanded production, increases remuneration for work and social benefits.

Lack of Freedom of Choice

So much for the provisions and promises in all the recent constitutions on paper. Altogether missing, even on paper, is the individual's freedom to choose as a natural right, as a consumer, producer, and entrepreneur. But actual practice is far worse. Individuals have no freedom of choice in the type and place of work, even the part of the country in which to reside; nor do they have free choice in education or training. They have no freedom to travel. They may not marry without permission or have children without allotment. Their lives are circumscribed by resident's certificates, ration cards for staples and clothing, and permits of all kinds that can be and are withheld or withdrawn by the Party as a means of control. Hence the individual is a tool, a cog in the machine of national, socialist planning. Furthermore, the Party may choose at any time either to tighten or to relax its administrative controls. Laws and regulations may be enacted to define the severity of such controls but their interpretation is in the hands of the Communist Party. At any rate, rules can be changed even more quickly than constitutions have been. The Party sometimes dispenses with legal niceties in the interest of swiftness and convenience of those in control. Hence the human cog is caught in the Party machine and must endure its fate in accordance with how Party leaders deal with their priorities and the nature of the problems they face.

It is hard to imagine for a citizen of a free country what all this means in practice. Every so often a visitor from abroad has been observed to ask a young Chinese what he or she wanted to become in life, only to be surprised by the answer obvious for such a system: that he or she would go where sent to by the government and do what the government wanted.

Forced Labor as Punishment and "Education"

The individual's rights as a producer in the People's Republic are affected most by compulsion in work assignment on a broad scale. the severity of this practice varies from job assignment by the government to long sentences in "reform through labor" or "education through labor" establishments (and mobile contingents of the same).

"Reform through labor" as a penal institution and policy was literally celebrated in a Chinese journal on legal studies in 1983 in which the author of the article praised the underlying philosophy of changing a person's outlook through a combination of work and education.[8] In reality, the practice started at the very beginning of the Chinese communist regime when forced labor under confined conditions (prison or labor camp) or in mobile contingents became a part of the sentence meted out in the beginning of the 1950s to those "counter-revolutionaries" who were not put to death outright. The Labor Reform Law itself, republished in the post-Mao period, was first promulgated by the State Administrative Council in September 1954.[9] Both ordinary criminals and counter-revolutionaries have to work without pay during the entire length of their sentence. Their production is integrated into the national economic plan (Article 30); their activities are planned and managed at different governmental levels and include both current industrial, mining and agricultural activities and large infrastructure projects in, for instance, water conservancy and road building (Article 33). Mobilization plans involving this labor force are drafted by the Ministry of Public Security at the central government level--not requiring higher level approval if the number of persons involved is small (not defined) and their transfer is only for short periods.

"Education through labor," on the other hand, was initially a different program. It was institutionalized in 1957 under a government decision formally approved by the NPC Standing Committee on August 1 of that year. The decision was republished on February 26, 1980 to remind the public of its currency and appears in the same legal compendium of that year as the Reform through Labor law mentioned above. Under this decision, "the police, other government agencies, organizations, enterprises, schools and other units, or parents and guardians" (Article 211) can apply to higher government authorities or their appointed agents for the commitment of individuals to "education through labor" establishments. The period of commitment varies from one to three years and may be extended for a fourth year. The potential candidates of compulsory labor in this category are vagrants, disturbers of the peace, individuals expelled by their schools or places of employment (who are without means of livelihood), persons who can, but for a prolonged period would not, work and workers who breach discipline and create public disorder, as well as those who do not accept their job assignments or transfers.[10] In addition, counter-revolutionaries not being further prosecuted for criminal responsibilities and persons who have been dismissed for their anti-socialism and who have no other means of livelihood are subject to education through labor.[11] Work under these "administrative measures" is paid.

In a statement dated February 29, 1980, the State Council allowed that an increase in the number of persons moving from one place to another, apparently illegally, and of minor crimes after 1961, a year of severe food shortage and economic crisis in the aftermath of the Great Leap, was successfully dealt with by public security agencies by means of "compulsory labor" and "detention pending investigation." Since the objects of these measures coincided with those of "education through labor," the government then decided to fold the several separate systems into a single institution of "education through labor." This part of the PRC's forced labor contingents, generally speaking, is not composed of persons currently serving criminal sentences. It is made up by what Marx would have called the army of the unemployed, plus dissidents and other troublemakers who by virtue of their activities and possible dismissal from their jobs may also have joined the ranks of the unemployed. Many dissidents connected with the "Democratic Wall" are known to have been sentenced to "education through. labor." The "education through labor" camps were initiated in 1957 when accelerated collectivization in the previous year had increased the flux of rural population into open urban unemployment. They originated in part from the pressure of social unrest which the unemployed and others caused. These camps have supplied a partial answer to the PRC's post-Mao unemployment problem. (See Appendix.)

The other part of the PRC's forced labor contingents working without pay corresponds essentially to the population serving time in prison or labor camps or in mobile labor contingents. The original members of this group were the same as those serving time under the 1954 law.

In September 1980, the Supreme People's Court reported that of some 1.2 million cases handled by the nation's courts during the Cultural Revolution,[12] 1.13 million cases had been reviewed through June 1980. Of those reviewed, 270,000 involved counter-revolution-aries; the others allegedly were ordinary criminal cases. The Court further reported changes in judgments, implying reversals and case dismissals, in 175,000 counter-revolutionary cases involving 184,000 persons and 76,000 other cases involving 82,000 persons. These

figures offer a rough indication of the umber of persons
that may have been added to the "reform through labor"
contingents over roughly a decade, not counting those
incarcerated without being recorded or having never even
gone through the regular courts. The number of counter-
revolutionary cases said to contain errors represented
an average of 64 percent of those reviewed--the ratio
was as high as 70-80 percent in some areas. This is
further proof of the role divergence of opinion, trumped
up charges and the like play in such political trials.
These figures do not include the "prison" population at
the beginning of the above accounting period or
attrition through deaths and releases during the period
and besides may very well contain reported cases only
from some cities.

Residents' Registration and "Non-persons"

The majority of Chinese workers probably accept
their assigned jobs because they have no alternative.
Farmers, like serfs, are tied to their rural lives
because they are not free to move to the cities. Urban
residents cannot move to other cities because they have
to have jobs to which they are not officially
transferred. What happens when the rules are disobeyed
or challenged?

Available reports indicate that from time to time
individuals sequestered in the various types of forced
labor institutions escape and that some escapees even
manage to return to their original places of
residence.[13] When such occurrences increased greatly in
number in recent years, the NPC Standing Committee was
called upon to issue a Decision on the methods to deal
with escapees from "labor reform" and "labor education."
A measure commonly followed by the local public security
organs in such cases, according to reports from
different parts of the country, is to cancel the
"residents' registrations" in the original localities of
the persons in question.[14] As a means of general control the residents' registration system has been used to
check population movement. A person not properly registered in a particular locality cannot receive rationed
goods, including staple foods and clothing, or become
legally employed. He or she becomes a "non-person" who
must eke out an existence in the underworld.

A person going to a government-ordered job
assignment in a different locality is often separated
from his/her family for long periods. Reuniting husband
and wife, not to mention other family members, is
stimied by bureaucratic indifference and by many local
authorities' unwillingness to make the necessary
residents' registration adjustments. This is true
especially if a person who is a registered rural
resident desires to move to an urban area. A newspaper
in South China reported on October 29, 1980, that 72

couples were separated in this manner among the faculty members of one single college.[15] Applications for a move to reunite married couples, it said, could not be approved in less than three to five years. In one of these 72 cases thirty years had passed since the husband's first effort to have his wife join him. A national meeting on this topic as it affected the country's cadres was held in November 1980. The participants assembled in Peking agreed to make adjustments in 22,000 cases. The total number of applications was not cited.

The plight of technical cadres, as in the last example, has caught the eyes of PRC leaders pursuing their modernization program. Inability to gain legal residence status has also plagued the rural population. Women and children have been affected especially harshly. Women have been refused legal residence when they try to return to their parental households after divorce. Rural women married to urban residents who wish to remain in the country--perhaps through inability to find housing--have had their original legal residence cancelled. Some woman workers lose their residents' registrations upon marriage simply because the rural authorities fear that they may become pregnant and therefore can no longer work.[16] Retired persons, persons returning home after completing forced labor sentences, and even the family members of persons officially assigned to work in rural areas have often been refused the status of legal residence. The children of women who are non-persons become themselves non-persons. In some localities, according to a December 1982 report of the Ministry of Public Security,[17] infants born "outside the plan" are not allowed to become legal residents and are therefore non-persons. Separation of families is sometimes a punishment under the birth control program for having too many children.

The explicit promises of the PRC constitution to protect the family and to provide special care for mother and child are contradicted by actual practice in providing work and employment. But this is not all.

Birth Control by Bureaucrats and Neighbors

Nowhere are the rights of individual Chinese citizens more vitally and intimately affected by the country's economic planning as it affects population growth and personal consumption. As mentioned earlier, the 1982 constitution extolls socialist economic planning. According to the sixth five-year plan (1981-85), the target of per capita annual consumption for 1985 will be 277 yuan (approximately $126 at the May 1984 rate of one yuan to $0.4559). If attained, this would be ¥50 higher than in 1980, representing an annual increase of 4.1 percent.[18] The plan's chance of success very much depends upon the rate of population growth, which was at 14.55 per thousand in 1981.[19] (The birth rate was 20.91 per thousand that year.) The plan calls for a total population not exceeding 1.06 billion in 1985 or keeping the birth and natural growth rates within 19 per thousand and 13 per thousand respectively. The latter rates were exceeded by those of 1981. Since the population on July 1, 1982, was already 1,008,175,000 according to the preliminary estimate of the census of that year, an almost immediate drop of natural growth to the plan target for 1985 would be necessary if the population targets for 1985 are to be reached. What have the post-Mao leaders done about this problem and why have they opted for the specific measures they have chosen?

Chapter 29 of the sixth plan, which deals with this demographic problem, lists four principal tasks: propaganda and education, the energetic advocacy of one child per family, technical assistance in planned parenthood, and institutional and personnel development. Central to the entire policy is "a significant increase in the ratio of one-pregnancy couples, strict control of second births, and elimination of multiple births "principally through education," supplemented by necessary economic, <u>administrative and organizational measures</u>" (underline added). Furthermore, the planners speak of instituting a "planned parenthood responsibility system" that would be appropriate to the kind of production responsibility system, of which variant forms exist, practiced in agriculture in a given area. Finally, cadres will be assigned at the basic level to function as specialists in this matter. What do all these measures really entail?

A set of detailed rules was adopted by the Standing Committee of the Kwangtung (Kwangtong) Provincial People's Congress in South China in February 1980.[20] Young people are encouraged to marry late by restricting entry to educational institutions at the middle and higher levels, as well as apprenticeship training, to the unmarried; by granting cash subsidies or exemptions from payment of school fees and medical expenses to couples of child-bearing age who have only one child, in addition to other forms of preferential treatment; by imposing increasingly heavier financial and other penalties on those who have more than one child. The penalties include demanding reimbursement of subsidies previously received, special taxes and fees, denial of rations, higher prices for staples supplied by the state, exclusion from consideration for job assignment, etc. (See also Chapter 3 for some of the social effects.)

Most notable, however, is a statement in these regulations that requires the rural commune and the local district in towns to review and approve the list of local women permitted to become pregnant on the basis of plan targets handed down by higher authorities. This constitutes a priority or waiting list which the local citizens must observe in giving birth to children and which the local officials administer.

Although the Kwangtung regulations have no open provision on compulsory abortion, periods of rest of varying legnths are allowed in cases of induced miscarriage and mid-term termination of pregnancy. In this connection reference can be made to a public television showing to a large U.S. audience of the model birth control program of Changzhou in Kiangsu (Jiangsu) Province (not far from Shanghai) in 1984.[21] The film was made with the express permission and obvious encouragement of PRC authorities for it included a scene of award giving and celebration among the cadres when the local target of one-birth families was met. The same film also showed how a woman in advanced pregnancy was under the incessant pressure of cadres and their agents (many being neighbors) in the district residents' organization and was subjected in the end to involuntary abortion. How women whose turns to have children had been changed had their names shifted by the monitors was graphically demonstrated in the film. The individual's privacy and human dignity are totally disregarded as Chinese planners pursue the solution of their demographic problem. The Chinese Communist Party and its bureaucracy have thus arrogated to themselves the additional power to decide who is to be born.

Perils at the Marketplace

Draconian population controls are but one of the twin blades used in cutting the knot that threatens to stop economic growth. Increase in production would be the other. This, in the eyes of the present PRC leaders, is to be accomplished in part by opening up the economy to Western capital, enterprise, and technology and in part by loosening up and enlivening the socialist system. The last part of these reforms is clearly indicated in the sixth five-year plan which calls for the expansion of cooperatives, i.e., collectively owned enterprises, and individual proprietorships.[22] Both state and collective enterprises are called upon to assist the individual proprietors through subcontracting, credit and supply of materials. How far these developments can go before coming into conflict with the economic dominance of the state sector, the trappings of socialism and the Communist Party's political dictatorship has been a source of constant uncertainty.

This uncertainty is inherent in the conflict between centralist planning and the market system. It is inevitable as a result of experimentation, as well as the back and forth swing of economic measures that reflect the political struggle among factions at the top and their differences. The severe impact on the rights of individuals in their economic pursuits, however, is largely a result of the habitual response of PRC leaders to those domestic developments that they view as a threat. (See Chapters 3 and 4.)

A strong official demonstration of concern that the communist system was being threatened by developing economic changes came from the Standing Committee of the Fifty National People's Congress on March 8, 1982 when it decided to modify 13 articles in the only recently adopted criminal code.[23] Changes were also made in the criminal law procedure.[24] In general, these changes have had the effect of lengthening prison sentences, making imposition of the death sentence easier and faster, and reducing the chance of appeal for a review. The decision was followed a month later by a joint decision of the State Council and the CCP Central Committee, which, while echoing the NPC's intention to punish perpetrators of economic crimes, pointed to ambiguities and imperfections in some of the new economic measures and spoke of more lenient treatment for those who confessed.[25] However, newspapers in 1983 continued to contain reports on death sentences for smuggling, breaching of exchange controls, misappropriation of public property, offers and taking of bribes, and other "economic crimes."[26] According to these sporadically publicized examples, death sentences were imposed on alleged criminals whose profits from crime were by Western standards as low as ¥38,000 ($17,300) for embezzlement, ¥42,200 ($19,000) for smuggling, and ¥130,000 ($59,300) for misappropriation, accumulated sometimes over a period of years. According to Premier Zhao Ziyang, both the Sixth NPC and the Twelfth Central Committee of the CCP took pains in late 1983 to combat "the tendency towards bourgeois liberalism in the cultural and ideological spheres."[27]

The issues involved are not merely whether the severity of a crime and its punishment match each other. The punishments are aimed at problems which are not necessarily crimes in a different society, even a different Chinese context, but which to the PRC authorities have to be resolved. Individual behavior at the marketplace and its side effect present PRC rulers with intractible problems. From the point of view of this chapter an outstanding issue in the Chinese treatment of "spiritual pollution" is the readiness with which authorities at every level resort to changing their own laws and trampling on established procedure. Their excuse is the need to resolve serious immediate problems. In doing so, however, they violate the rights of their own citizens whom they claim they wish to protect. This is an outcome of long practice and betrays a particular thought and behavior pattern which the CCP shares with other authoritarian governments.

Systemic Conflicts in Shaping New Economic Policies?

Following the tightening of political control through punitive measures of the kind described above, Zhao Ziyang has announced new economic measures aimed at increasing efficiency and productivity.[28] Each of these measures, however, has far-reaching implications that can come into basic conflict with one or another of Deng's cardinal principles on socialism and Communist Party dictatorship.

First, the "responsibility system" introduced earlier in agriculture allows the farmer to contract to supply a fixed amount to the state and the collective, for which he is held "responsible," and to dispose of the balance as he sees fit. A similar system is now applied to industrial enterprises. The latter are to pay preset taxes instead of turning over their entire profits to the state. Other measures include the expansion of the scope of the individual economy in which private entrepreneurs are permitted to make their own production decisions and to be responsible for their own profit and loss and for making production, cost, sales, pricing, investment, and payroll plans. After paying their taxes, the enterprises are to dispose of their after-tax profits. To that extent, therefore, they will be free to make investments out of retained earnings although their other investment funds, which they have to obtain from and pay back to the Construction Bank, now replacing the Treasury, are still nominally governed by the central plan. In distribution, goods are to be sold both wholesale and retail through multiple channels once government purchases have been satisfied. The scale of wages which varies by skill will do away with egalitarianism. Moreover, the encouragement of joint ventures with foreign business has been reinforced by the addition of 14 more coastal urban centers to the Special Economic Zones in which similar enterprises and businesses of sole foreign ownership can be established. The general tenor of these policies is to provide more material incentive, to enhance efficiency through decentralization in decision making, to free pricing and encourage the market system, and to increase the inflow of foreign technology and capital while expanding exports. Finally, Zhao wants the intellectuals to be given more material consideration and general respect and to be allowed greater participation in decision making so that modernization can proceed further.

The risks to the Chinese Communist authorities and Party will increase with the degree of success of these policies. A substantial expansion of the individual economy and of independently determined production and investment activities could divert resources away from the planned state sector and threaten the government's control over resources and their use. Relaxing control in material allocation would make such unwanted changes easier. The goernment may then be compelled to compete for resources through expanding the budget and inflation, which already is becoming a problem.

The success of individual entrepreneurs could--some say will inevitably--adversely affect income distribution and rekindle class differences. Once increased private income can no longer be spent entirely on larger personal consumption, ownership of private property may expand into investments in other businesses than one's own.[29] The separation of ownership from use of property in production may no longer be tenable and the right to inheritance may extend beyond personal property and residential housing. This would obviously weaken the government's control over the individual by controlling his or her means of livelihood. A Chinese bourgeoisie might then re-emerge.

Finally, what affects the individual economy and the private citizen is bound to affect members of the Party vanguard and the military. It may then become difficult to keep the Party and the military free from impure, non-socialist thought or "spiritual pollution." Besides, co-opted intellectuals and returned students from the West may join successful business entrepreneurs, as well as members of a modernized military-political cadre, to challenge the old-line Communist Party's monopoly of power.

In the long run, therefore, success of these economic policies will threaten, first, socialism and then the political dictatorship of the Communist Party which are among Deng Xiaoping's minimal conditions economic reform must observe as outer bounds. The availability of new economic opportunities will weaken the power, prestige and attractiveness (as jobs) of the PLA and the Communist Party bureaucracy. Those who are most successful in the private sector may also be among those most oppressed under the former tight economic control because they have least to lose.

An alternative is to prevent these measures from being too successful--which may not be at all difficult. To do so PRC authorities need only to intensify once more the punitive measures against human rights they know so well, but at a cost to economic well-being. A third alternative is for the PRC to be lucky enough to obtain for an indefinite period sufficient external assistance which will offset the inefficiency a half-hearted economic reform--that is, one not thorough enough to undermine the Communist Party's dictatorship--will still leave. The last alternative is not up to the Chinese alone. It is improbable not only because outside help, however willingly proffered by the West and Japan, each for its own reasons, will not likely prove enough, but also because such help and its benefits are unlikely to be wisely and efficiently used and diffused within a communist framework. Between the first two scenarios, the behavior of the Chinese public will be decisive. Will it honestly accept the Communist Party line and "love the Communist Party" heart and soul? (See Chapter 6.) The answer depends upon ideology and conviction.

There clearly are powerful elements in the Communist Party who not only prefer the second alternative but believe that the cost to economic efficiency will be tolerable. They are likely to be encouraged in this thinking if they perceive Western capital and technology to be forthcoming in sufficient quantity and over a long enough period to help them muddle through and maintain the dictatorship of the Communist Party. They may of course be mistaken and will not then be able to avoid a crisis, economic and political, in the end.

ENDNOTES

1. For the text of the 1948 UN Universal Declaration, see Everyone's United Nations, a Handbook on the United Nations, Its Structure and Activities (New York: United Nations, 1968), 8th edition, Appendices, pp. 412-415.

2. For articles cited in the text, ibid., pp. 416-423.

3. The English text used below is taken from China Reconstructs (Beijing), March 1975, pp. 10-15.

4. The original text is from the Library of Congress, Far Eastern Law Division.

5. The English text of the 1978 constitution employed here is that of the Foreign Language Press, Beijing, 1978, first edition.

6. The English text of the 1982 constitution used here is that of Xinhua, Beijing, December 4, 1984.

7. The Code was adopted on July 1, 1979, by the Fifth NPC during its second session and became effective on January 1, 1980. For a complete Chinese text, see Office of Policy and Legal Research, Ministry of Public Security, Gongan Faguei Huibian (Compendium of Public Security Laws), (Beijing: Qunzhong Publishers, 1980), pp. 6-33. Chapter III of Part II deals with crimes against the socialist economic order but should be read in conjunction with Chapter I which treats "crimes of counter-revolution."

8. Liu Qing, "Xin Zhongguo di Laodong Gaizao Zuifan Zhihdu" (On the Reform through Labor System of New China), in Fazhih (Legal Studies), No. 4, Beijing, August 23, 1983. For a complete overview of the laws against counter-revolutionaries, see Gongan Faguei Huibian of 1980 cited above, pp. 93-109.

9. This was proclaimed on September 7, 1954. For a complete text in English, see Albert P. Blaustein, ed., Fundamental Legal Documents of Communist China (South Hackensack, N.J.: Fred B. Rothman Co., 1962), pp. 240-265. The Chinese text is in Gongan Faguei Huibian, 1980, pp. 195-206.

10. In a 1982 case, a graduate of a South China college of agriculture who refused to accept a job assignment had his resident's registration

transferred by the school authorities to his place of birth. (His food ration card went with it.) He was also barred for five years from employment in any state enterprise. Nanfang Ribao (Canton), August 5, 1980.

11. The State Council's Decision on "Education through Labor," originally published on August 3, 1957, was republished on February 26, 1980. The complete Chinese text can be found in Gongan Faguei Huibian, 1980, pp. 209-211.

12. Nanfang Ribao, September 17, 1980, p. 2.

13. According to a December 7, 1981, report of the Supreme Procuratorate, statistics from 18 cities only showed that in one month 800 "education through labor" escapees either gave themselves up or were returned by their parents while another 1,600 escapees from both "education" and "reform" through labor were caught by the authorities. Nanfang Ribao, December 16, 1981, p. 3.

14. See, for instance, reports in the Renmin Ribao, (Beijing) September 8, 1981, p. 4 and August 8, 1981, p. 1; the Nanfang Ribao, September 11 and 19, 1981, pp. 1 and 3 respectively.

15. The Nanfang Ribao, November 6, 1980, p. 3.

16. The Nanfang Ribao, January 18, 1982, p. 2.

17. These details are contained in a report to the State Council and published in abstract form in the Guowuyuan Gongbao (State Council Bulletin) No. 21, (1982), February 12, 1983, pp. 1026-1028.

18. A summary report of the sixth national economic development plan is contained in the Guowuyuen Gongbao of June 10, 1983, No. 9,pp. 393-394 and 398-399.

19. "Bulletin on the Principal Findings of the 1982 Census," Bureau of Statistics, dated October 27, 1982; Guowuyuen Gongbao, No. 17, December 10, 1982, pp. 746-750.

20. The Kwangtung regulations are contained in a lengthy report in the Nanfang Ribao of February 13, 1980. For the detailed rules on compulsory sterilization and granting of dispensation for second pregnancies, see the same paper, January 5 and June 17, 1983. For instance, if a second child has been born to a couple since 1979, either the

man or the woman must be sterilized. On the other hand, a commune member who "really experiences difficulties" (meaning unexplained) and has only one daughter can petition the brigade, commune, and county authorities--all three--for permission to have a second pregnancy.

It should be noted that no nationwide general regulations in equal detail have apparently been made publicly available and that strict controls of the kind enforced in Kwangtung are not applied to certain areas inhabited by minority nationalities.

21. The film was shown in the science program (NOVA) by a Public Television station (Channel 9) in San Francisco on February 14, 1984; excerpts were shown on the nationwide CBS "60 Minutes" program two days earlier.

22. See the plan summary in the Guowuyuan Gongbao, No. 9, June 10, 1983, pp. 395-396.

23. For the text of the NPC Standing Committee Decision, see the Guowuyuan Gongbao, No. 6, April 30, 1982, 203-206. The Criminal Code provisions affected are Articles 118, 146, 148, 152, 155, 157, 162, 171, 173, 185, 187, 188, and 190.

24. See Sichuan Ribao (Chengdu), September 4, 1983, p. 3.

25. See the Guowuyuan Gongbao, No. 8, June 10, 1982, pp. 307-315.

26. These reports are contained in the Renmin Ribao, October 7, 1983, p. 4 and the Nanfang Ribao, September 29, 1983, p. 1, and again the Renmin Ribao, August 30, 1983, p. 4. Other similar reports abound from different parts of the country.

27. See Zhao Ziyang, "Report on the Work of the Government," delivered at the second Session of the Sixth NPC, May 15, 1984, Beijing Review (Beijing), Vol. 27, No. 24, June 11, 1984, p. II.

28. Zhao, ibid, pp. III-X.

29. See the reported purchase by Chinese of "stocks" issued by a South China state owned enterprise in The Wall Street Journal, July 19, 1984, p. 31.

6
Control of the Mind

All the constitutions of the People's Republic of China contain in their sections on fundamental rights and duties of citizens articles that promise freedom of speech, of the press, of assembly, of association, of procession and of demonstration, as well as religion. The first post-Mao constitution of 1978 also granted the people the right to "speak out, air views fully, hold great debates and write big character posters," as did the Maoist constitution of 1975, but attempted to alter and redirect the practices that had become popular during the Cultural Revolution into avenues of protest against Mao and Hua Guofeng, Mao's heir after the Gang of Four. Both post-Mao constitutions added the freedom to engage in research and artistic creation.

However, it was not said but clearly understood, that exercise of these freedoms must be within the confines of the communist system. In the post-Mao period this meant submission to Deng's Four Cardinal Principles--literally the "Four Minimum Requirements." These are: the leadership of the Chinese Communist Party; the Socialist Road; the Dictatorship of the Proletariat; Marxism-Leninism and the Thought of Mao Zedong. "Constitutional freedoms" can therefore never be used in opposition to communism. What is specifically forbidden or how the above is interpreted can vary greatly according to the party line of the moment. Stepping over the line brings calamity, particularly the accusation of being a counter-revolutionary. It will result in punishment of varying degrees, including death. Expressing thought that the Party regards as opposed to its line of the time is regarded as a counter-revolutionary act.

Free to Think?

It was generally known by Chinese in the past that the individual was required to go beyond being submissive and pliant. It was not enough to avoid opposing the Party openly; it was necessary openly to express support of the Party. In so-called study

77

sessions at work, in schools and neighborhoods, and in any and every group, the latest Party directives and speeches by leaders were discussed under the guidance of Party cadres. It was vital for each participant to proclaim full support, which was best and most safely expressed bu parroting or paraphrasing the original documents as closely as possible. Witholding of enthusiastic support would be regarded as indication of a hostile attitude towards the official position. When a person came under attack for deviation from the Party line, it was the duty of the others, locally or nationally according to the importance of the case, to join in the condemnation, lest they themselves fall victim to the same calumny. There was no freedom of silence.

For a while after Mao, this practice was thought to have been discontinued. But when writers and essayists came under fire for bourgeois liberalism in late 1983, many intellectuals panicked and found it necessary to join the chorus by coming out with their supporting stand as before. A special Chinese term, biaotai, to take a public position, has been used to characterize this assumption of protective coloring for survival's sake.

Shedding the Burden of Mao

There had been after all a bitter experience in the past. During the "hundred flower" movement of 1956 when intellectuals and "democratic personalities" were encouraged by Mao to comment critically on the Communist Party's policies up to that time, those who took Mao at his word found themselves later targets of vilification and severe punishment. The slogan "let the hundred flowers bloom," which was to indicate the freedom and plurality of thought, soon became transformed into a trap sprung on the unsuspecting whose ideas had become "poisonous weeds" to the Party leadership. Many of the intellectual victims in 1956 were members of the non-communist coalition parties represented in the Political Consultative Conference which had been used by the Communist Party in the early years to give its government the semblance of a coalition. This group, long in oblivion during Mao's ascendancy, has been resuscitated by post-Mao leaders to serve the same purpose. Remembering the nightmares of the past, they were understandably afraid and not about to repeat their mistake. In a public meeting at the end of October 1983, when their opinions on Communist Party rectification and policy were solicited, they simply joined in condemning juvenile delinquency, liberal bourgeois concepts and corrupt ideologies, not daring to raise any critical voice against any Party policy, past or present. Any potential voice of open criticism has long been silenced; in its place only apathy and mistrust remain.

The Party's insistence on conformity is based on its position that it alone is the fountain of truth. In the tortured logic of the Marxist-Leninist interpretation of history truth is what serves the realization of the march of history toward the assumed communist millenium, and since the Communist Party is the vanguard in the march, it is by definition the possessor of truth. Not to follow the Party line, let alone to oppose it, is not only wrong but is counter-revolutionary and criminal. When reality is in such contrast with the claims of the Party lines' success, the obvious consequence is disillusionment and loss of faith. Chinese Communists in the post-Mao period have experienced this general reaction which they have admitted by calling it a "crisis of confidence."

Since it is vital for the maintenance of communist power to retain doctrinal sanction, the decline of authority of the doctrine can be lethal. To restore what can be salvaged requires the shedding of the symbols of past failure. The historical burden could not be shaken off simply by attributing all wrongs to the Gang of Four. The real burden is Mao Zedong.

How to treat Mao is, however, not a simple matter. In the first post-Mao succession when Hua Guofeng replaced the Gang of Four, Mao was needed by Hua to legitimize his seizure of power. Mao's alleged bestowal of the mantel of authority with the ambiguous statement "With you in charge I am at ease" was widely publicized in pictorial form, showing the two figures seated, with Mao's hand placed on Hua's knee. To strengthen his descendancy from Mao, Hua in great haste had constructed the Mao mausoleum so as to encapsulate Maoism symbolically. Aside from the unusual monarchical anointment procedure, in retrospect, Hua blundered in linking himself to the very aspect of Maoism that had lost its credibility. Mao's assumption of sole authority to make all decisions for the Party was at the heart of the Mao cult now in disrepute. The communist doctrine had to be separated from it. The personality cult of Mao, surpassing by far that of Stalin, became condemned as "superstition," or "theology," and separated by other Party leaders from true socialism. On the other hand, Mao was still needed by the Chinese Communist Party whose whole history is so intertwined with Mao that any total condemnation of the former "helmsman" would disqualify the Party from continuing its rule. After all, each and every one of the present leaders was a follower of Mao at one time or another; and had at least tacitly supported Maoist policies and his cult. No hands were really clean.

What is more, the doctrine of Marxist-Leninism needs a Chinese image, lest it became a totally Western import. There is no other Chinese communist prophet who could take his place. For communist China the doctrine has to remain Marxism-Leninism-Mao Zedong Thought for a time at least. Since the inclusion of the proclaimed Thought of Mao in the Trinity of Chinese communism is symbolic rather than substantive, an elaboration of its content is avoided. This abstention leaves the way open for reinterpretation and additions of doctrinal tenets.

Can Socialism be Wrong?

One attempt to explain away the horrors of the Maoist past, in particular, of the Cultural Revolution, was to postulate that even under socialism there could be "alienation" which in Marxist terminology means an inherent force that undermines itself and was applied by Marx to capitalism only. In fact, this concept was used by prominent Party members to try and explain how and why things could have gone so wrong. However, the advocates of this propositon were immediately met with scorn and with demand for recantation like heretics. Democratic centralism did not leave room for freedom of thought within the party itself, even after Mao's death.

The most outstanding known victims were the director and editor-in-chief of the People's Daily, who were dismissed, and Zhou Yang who had been for a long time under Mao an arbiter for the Party in literary matters and had himself been responsible for accusations against many writers and their eventual purge. Now Zhou had come to speak of alienation under socialism in the economic, political and ideological fields in order to explain away the "many foolish things" of the past. Harshly taken to task, he was forced to undergo self criticism and recant. Self-criticism, the public confession of how one has erred and deviated from the truth, was used extensively in Maoist time to enforce conformity. It obviously still is a proper tool to maintain the official monopoly of truth.

Social Relations versus Individual Rights

In order to salvage the good reputation of socialism the claim has also been made by Zhou Yang and others that humanism was not incompatible with socialist theory. According to this view, the early Marx was a humanist. Marxist "humanitarianism" was therefore part of socialism. This humanist reinterpretation of socialism had been struck down by no lesser a personage than Hu Qiaomu, the theorist guru of the Party under Deng Xiaoping, in a lengthy speech on January 3, 1984. [1]

In Hu's official interpretation, man can only be evaluated in connection with his relation to society. There are no independent human values such as human dignity and human freedom, or in fact any other human right. This is tantamount to denying all the human rights ostensibly guaranteed in the 1982 and earlier constitutions and coincides with our interpretation of the Communist Party's attitude all along.

No More "Democracy Wall"

The reaction to the inhumanities of the Cultural Revolution took a much stronger course outside the Party than these feeble attempts to provide the Chinese Communist Party with a doctrinally more human face. Popular criticism went much deeper. This was already apparent in the vast Tienanmen Square protest meeting in April 1976 in which for the first time Mao and Jiang Qing were personally attacked. This mass rally, first described as "counter-revolutionary," was under the post-Mao regime recognized as having been "revolution-ary," although its anti-Mao character is no longer publicized. The practical de-Maoization of policy, after Deng had seized power, opened the gates to pent-up emotions. Both expectations and protests mounted. In the recent tradition of the wall posters of the Cultural Revolution large numbers of the young generation in Peking expressed their feelings in handbills, posters, essays and pamphlets plastered on what became known as the "Democracy Wall" at Xidan in Peking. Privately circulated journals appeared in growing numbers, one of the most famous being Tan Suo (Exploration), edited by the best known of the dissidents, Wei Jingsheng, a young electrician who had been a Red Guard, self-educated and widely read. (See Chapter 4.) These publicized ideas on the Democracy Wall and in the dissident journals raised a whole program of demands for freedom, beginning with the call for human rights.[2] The feeling was that "a new epoch had come," and the goal was "prosperity, wealth, democracy and freedom." Some attacked Mao as having been "more vicious than the first emperor," indeed had topped all tyrants. Everyone had lived in constant fear, they charged. Now "the autocratic system has been overthrown and the autocrat has died." Today "the need for genuine democracy and human rights is greater than ever." A few of the writers of the wall-papers went so far as to demand a multi-party system modelled after the democracies of the West. (See also Chapters 3 and 4.)

Of the dissidents Wei Jingsheng became best known abroad. His accounts of conditions in a prison for political prisoners near Peking under the caption "Real Death," describing the cruelty and mental and physical tortures in prison, provided the first insight into this aspect of the communist system. His conclusion: "Marxist humanism does not exist."[3] Wei's essay on the "fifth modernization" described the plight and backward-ness of China, condemned communism as utopian, and concluded with the call for political modernization and democracy. Equally famous has become the transcript of Wei's defense in court, when he was accused of treason and condemned to 15 years in prison. At the time Lui Qing, the organizer of the April 5th Forum, another political group, was arrested for printing and distributing a tape of the court hearings. Another dissident, Hu Ping, a student at Peking University, became first known for his long and carefully argued essay on freedom of speech, as a modern fulcrum that would provide the stand by which everyone, like the Greek mathematician Archimedes, could move the world.

What was impressive about these and other young writers was their knowledge of Western literature, of Thomas Campanello's City of the Sun, Robert Owen's A New View of Society and many of the classics of Western political thought. In an unattributed article on human rights of January 1, 1979, the author demanded democracy pure and simple, with the division of powers according to Montesquieu's l'ésprit des lois, with law, a constitution, voting rights, freedom of speech, freedom to demonstrate by one's own volition, freedom of public action, freedom of beliefs - all beliefs, listing Buddhism, Islam, Christianity, Taoism, Marxism and Pragmatism - and freedom of association. In January 1979, the China Human Rights League was founded and drew up a "Nineteen Point" list of demands, calling for free expression of views, elections, open government, racial justice, the right to travel and basic economic rights.

At first the government's attitude was one of tolerance. In fact, one can assume that the condemnation of Maoist past was of use to Deng Xiaoping in his effort to remove Hua Guofeng and company from power. When they were no longer needed, Deng turned against the dissidents. In March 1979 the Party leadership's attitude towards the dissidents began to change. Deng soon after declared that they had gone too far in their demands.

The clamping down on expressions of discontent came by installment. On March 22, 1979, the People's Daily declared that "the worn out weapon of 'human rights' which has long been reactionary bourgeois dictatorship's window-dressing" could not be used as a "remedy for the problems of a socialist country." When shortly thereafter Wei Jingsheng criticized Deng Xiaoping personally, he was arrested. In December of the same year, Democracy Wall was closed to posters. In February 1980 the Party Central Committee rescinded the stipulations in the 1978 constitution that had granted (Article 45) the people the right "to speak out freely, air views fully, hold great debates and write big character posters." The final crackdown came in April of 1981 when the Central Committee ordered the suppression of "illegal organizations" and "illegal publications," leading to the arrest of a large number of dissidents and the banning of their journals.[4] The dissidents and the protests on the Democracy Wall had served their purpose; when they began to ask for true human rights from the people now in power, they were crushed.

Freedom of Religion

All Chinese communist constitutions since 1949 contained articles on freedom of religion as a right of the citizens. Nevertheless, churches and temples were destroyed, desecrated, or used for secular purposes; priests were imprisoned, some executed; and "the feudal system of suppression and exploitation which the religious temples and clergy practiced" was abolished. [5] Yet if the assumption that religion prospers in adversity has any validity, the case of China can offer an example. Religion was practiced in clandestine home churches and, according to some accounts, the number in the case of Christians at least has substantially increased, with estimates ranging from the official figure of six million to an unofficial estimate of ten to twenty million.[6]

In the post-Mao period the policy toward religion has had to face these realities. There was the growth of adherence to religion in spite of official oppression and discrimination. Minorities, especially in Tibet and Turkestan and among scattered groups in Southwest China had held on to their religions in spite of government policies to eradicate their beliefs. Finally, opening to the West at the beginning of the seventies invited Western concern about freedom of religion. For all these reasons the post-Mao regime has had to develop new approaches toward religion behind the facade of the constitutional guarantee of religious freedom.

The present attitude of the Communist Party in China seems to be that religious practices are better controlled when they are conducted openly and in organized groups with leaders who can be called to account. For this reason churches and temples have been opened, where alone religious activities are supposed to take place. To aid monitoring such activities, persons who attend religious services are required to carry special passes.[7] Altogether eight national associations of organized religious groups--three catholic, two protestant and one each for Buddhism, Islam and Taoism--have been established under government and Party control. The multiple Christian associations are functionally divided.

These religious bodies under Party and state control must not owe allegiance to any non-Chinese authority. This prohibition particularly affects the Catholic Church. Chinese catholics have been forced to sever their relations with the Vatican, and refusal to do so has meant a long continued imprisonment for many and reimprisonment for some. In this category are several Chinese bishops and clergymen, now in their seventies and eighties, who have been under arrest for many years for their constant loyalty to Rome. Papal infallibility in matters of the faith poses an additional challenge to Chinese communists from their perspective. The national Chinese Catholic Church in the PRC, which Rome does not recognize, has been forced to accede to the official policy of birth control and abortion, to reject papal infallibility and to continue its service in Latin, apparently to discourage mass participation.

Among other impediments there is the shortage of seminars, the official attitude of not permitting religious education for minors and the exclusion of all persons practicing religion from membership in the Communist Party and thereby from official careers and perquisites. In spite of all these handicaps religious activities have expanded rapidly under the new guidelines, a testimony to the irrepressibility of the human religious sentiment.

A special case is the persecution in Tibet, where church and state were one and where a Buddhist incarnation, the Dalai Lama, was the head of both. When Tibet fell under Beijing's control in 1951, the Chinese guaranteed not only freedom of religion but of all cultural and social tradition. Chinese rule, however, brought the worst case of violation of human rights in the early postwar period and led to the flight of the Dalai Lama and one hundred thousand Tibetans to India. Aside from the massive loss of life, the Maoist period left Tibet with a couple of dozens of temples and monasteries out of some three thousand before that. Post-Mao policy has permitted private restoration at no government cost of another dozen or more temples. The Tibetan people, who have remained deeply religious, are allowed to worship on certain days against the payment of a fee at restored temples which have been made into attractions for foreign tourists.[8] In late 1983, in line with the national drive against crime and counter-revolution, mass arrests and executions have been witnessed in Tibet, including priests.[9] But religious practice, both in Tibet and in the diaspora, has if anything actually increased.

In addition to the officially recognized organized religions, which have a body of doctrine, practices and organization, folk beliefs, such as geomancy, fortune telling, magic, and exorcism are condemned wholesale as "feudalistic" superstitions and as disruptive and subversive of social order and detrimental to economic progress. In answer to a reader's question on the difference between religious freedom and "feudalistic superstitious activity," a South China newspaper, Nanfang Ribao, stated on November 24, 1982, that feuda-listic superstitious activities are the means of profes-sionals to defraud others of money in answer to unresolved questions on the part of superstitious persons or to their prayers for relief from pain. The believers must follow their instructions which sometimes spread rumors, mislead the public, create contradictions

among clans, endanger social order, directly threaten
the security of life and property, and undermine the
spiritual civilization and construction of socialism.
    Therefore, the paper explained, the Party and the
government wished to protect proper religious activity
but prohibit and resolutely eradicate feudalistic
superstitions. The Communist Party's true concern in
this matter is, however, revealed in the September 2,
1983 Decision of the Sixth National People's Congress
Standing Committee on the severe punishment of criminals
posing a serious threat to social order. The Decision
raised the sentence normally imposed under the criminal
code for certain categories of crimes up to the level of
capital punishment. Among the categories of crimes to
which the Decision applies was the organization of
secret societies that engaged in counter-revolutionary
activities by taking advantage of feudalistic
superstitions to the serious detriment of social
order.[10] To those who know Chinese history, activities
through secret societies have always been the begin-
nings of organized political opposition.

Filling the Void with a New Faith
    The survival and revival of major religious faiths
and the irrepressible folk beliefs present both a
challenge and a threat to the regime. All attempts at
their management and containment have proved inadequate
both in the past and now. But the problem the regime
faces goes much deeper than it appears. After the
demotion of Mao, he has become the god that has failed.
The "crisis of confidence" that has been acknowledged by
the leadership cannot be overcome by the promise of a
materialistic utopia that remains elusive. How can the
gap be filled?
    In his speech of September 1982, Communist Party
chairman Hu Yaobang thought he had the answer.
Socialism, he claimed, had its own spiritual content
which he divided into cultural and ideological
aspects. [11] The cultural aspect of this spiritual
socialism is made up of such components as education,
science, art, literature, the media, recreation,
libraries, museums, and public health. The ideological
aspect of spiritual socialism consists of the Weltan-
schauung of the working class, scientific Marxism,
communist ideals, beliefs and moral values and "most of
all revolutionary ideals, morality and discipline."
This confused array of institutions, ideas and ideals
appears to be a naive attempt at taking refuge in a
crude form of idealism that "stands Marx on his head."
Marxist "superstructure" has become the underpinning of
Chinese socialism, in order to provide it with
"spiritualism" and to save it from the crisis of confidence. In terms of Mao's numbers game, there are "the
five stresses (decorum, manners, hygiene, discipline and

morals), the four beauties (mind, language, behavior and environment), and three loves (Party, motherland, and socialism)." [12] These slogans and others, like the "five good families" and new models of self-sacrifice, represent in more understandable non-communist language a Marxist parody of Confucian ethics. Confucian humanism (jen) and personal integrity (i) have been replaced by the love of Party, motherland and socialism and by new models of unselfish behavior. Hu's administrative colleague, Premier Zhao Ziyang, echoed these concepts in his report to the NPC on May 15, 1984. [13]

"Spiritual Pollution", Reflection of a Dilemma

If "spiritual socialism" were to prevail, it would have to be generally accepted to the exclusion of all competing values and ideas, originating from within or without. However, the broader the base of support the party seeks, the harder it becomes to maintain the monopoly of doctrinal interpretation of the social goals which the Party has presented as true values. To put the matter simply, will the people at large and intellectuals in particular love the Party, the motherland and socialism above all else? By opening China to the West ostensibly solely for the sake of technology and economic advantage, China can no longer keep up the barriers to ideas that challenge communist concepts. The impact of this flow of Western ideas is bound to increase with time as the number of Chinese of all levels exposed to them in China and abroad multiplies. China cannot indefinitely send tens and thousands of its intellectual elite abroad to study and open more and more cities and special economic zones to foreign enterprise and yet hope to quarantine the undesired ideas they bring in. Nor can the communist leaders prevent the reappearance of Chinese ethical values partly in response to outside stimulation.

The Party, however, continues to try to counter these "demoralizing" influences. The combination of a new life style in the cities, of new enterprises in the countryside, of a new freedom in art and literature and of the ideological challenge to socialist doctrine did bring in late 1983 an officially promoted nationwide drive against "spiritual pollution," in tandem with the suppression of economic crimes and social disorder while coinciding with the purge of the Party itself.

The target of "spiritual pollution" was defined by Deng Xiaoping in a speech before the CCP Central Committee in October 1983. He described "spiritual pollution" as the dissemination of "all varieties of corrupt and decadent ideologies of the bourgeoisie and other exploiting classes" and dissemination of "sentiments of distrust towards the socialist and communist cause and the Communist Party leadership."[14]

Deng's initiative was taken up by Party,
government and other groups throughout the country and
became a tool of action against ideological "deviation"
and literary and artistic freedom. The general attack
against the free spirit in politics and art was made
behind a screen of attack against moral corruption,
represented by "pornographic" material of all kinds
(rather broadly defined in China) which the Party held
responsible for contributing to juvenile deliquency.
When this drive led to attacks by radical Party members
against the life style of the young in the cities, such
as fashionable clothing, wearing of cosmetics, permanent
waves and high heels, and the money-making enterprises
of peasants in the countryside, the drive was curbed so
as not to interfere with the policy of modernization.
But the movement opposing "spiritual pollution" was
continued. An outstanding illustration of the
importance attributed to this ideological struggle was
provided by Premier Zhao Ziyang in his speech before the
National People's Congress on May 15, 1984. Zhao did
criticize the "inappropriate actions" taken in some
areas and by some units. According to him:

> "The people's demand for a better
> cultural and material life is justi-
> fied and should be encouraged and
> this should in no circumstances be
> confused with spiritual contamination
> on the ideological front." The
> contest between the enforcement of
> ideological conformity and free
> thought will obviously continue "for
> a long time to come."[15]

A key role in this continuing struggle will be
played by Chinese intellectuals, in China and abroad.
If the Chinese Communist Party leadership truly seeks
modernization, it must have in its employ larger and
larger numbers of educated people who can think for
themselves. This unavoidable development and the role
these persons play will be decisive in the conflict
between control and freedom of the mind.

ENDNOTES

1. Renmin Ribao, January 27, 1984, see FBIS No. 026, February 7, 1984, pp. K 1-33.

2. On the democracy wall see James Seymour (ed.), The Fifth Democratization (New York: Human Rights Publishing Group, 1980.)

3. See Tan Suo (Exploration), No. 3, March 11, 1979.

4. A fuller chronology of the events during this period can be found in Spearhead (New York: Bulletin of the Society for the Protection of East Asian's Human Rights), Vol. 19, Autumn, 1983.

5. U.S. Dept. of State, "Country Reports on Human Rights Practices for 1983," February 1983.

6. Ibid.

7. Ibid.

8. See Tibtan Review (New Dehli), especially March 1984, p. 7, April, 1984, p. 4; May, 1984 and June, 1984, pp. 10-13. For general complaints about the obstruction of local authorities to the restoration of the temples under the religious groups' own control, willfull destruction of historical religious texts, etc. See also the Hong Kong Ta Kung Pao, June 8, 1984.

9. Ibid.

10. Guowuyuan Gongbao, October 25, 1983, pp. 851-852. Reference should also be made to the Appendix on the rise in recent years of criminal cases involving disturbances of social order and the severe sentences meted out.

11. See Beijing Review, No. 18, May 2, 1983, pp. 18-19. A most interesting account of this subject can be found in a paper (unpublished) by Thomas B. Gold, "Just in Time!' China Battles Spiritual Pollution on the Eve of 1984," presented to the California Regional China Seminar, April, 1984.

13. Beijing Review, No. 24, June 11, 1984, p. 11.

14. Renmin Ribao, November 16, 1983, p. 1

15. Beijing Review, No. 24, June 11, 1984, p. 11.

7
Summing Up

Human rights are a key point of contention in the continuing confrontation between the Western tradition exalting individual freedom and Marxist-Leninist totalitarianism which finds granting such rights contradictory to their conception and style of political control. The issue of objectivity is almost always raised. Some claim that less should be expected from non-Western nations and even less from communist countries.

Every now and then, however, when gross violations of human rights occur that involve well-known personalities or are of a particularly outrageous nature--such as the shooting down of a Korean civilian airliner by a Soviet fighter, the attempted assassination of the Pope, the atrocities of the so-called Great Proletarian Cultural Revolution or the disclosures about the Gulag Archipelago--a public outcry is raised. But the echo soon dies. Lesser but numerous incidents occur daily and have had a benumbing influence. In fact the issue of human rights has become tiresome to many. To some it is no more than a political ploy in policy debates. Some see the splinter in the eye of a friend but fail to note the beam in the eye of the enemy. To others, while busy counting violations, the big, fundamental issue that must underlie a common global standard is easily forgotten. That is whether the organizing principles of a political system lend themselves to promoting or violating human rights.

Do the political system and economic policy of the People's Republic of China lend themselves to the protection of human rights? Has post-Mao China adopted goals that focus on the individual's rights, however much or little the condition of human rights has improved compared with the Maoist period? These are among the questions we have been trying to answer for post-Mao China. Another question is whether China's cultural past leads inevitably to policies that give low regard to the individual. Still another task we have undertaken is to look at the means of protecting human rights--which are absent in China--namely, a legal

89

system that is trusted and works. Finally, we're concerned with the nature, style and magnitude of human
rights violations and we are seeking an answer to the
question whether the situation in post-Mao China is in
some sense better than before, as many contend it is.

Regardless of the standards one employs, Mao's
abominable record in human rights is no longer in
dispute today. But what has happened after Mao? Has
post-Mao China moved away from the denial in principle
of the so-called "bourgeois" human rights of the West?
Or has there been at least a breach in the Chinese
Communist Party's old position, some wavering in its
stand? From the point of view of the future, not only
of China, but of the Marxist-Leninist system, the global
human rights cause, and U.S.-China relations, this question is of foremost importance. Assessment of what is
happening in China in the realm of human rights must, in
the final analysis, be a key factor in Western policy-
making. For the human race as a whole, what happens to
more than one billion fellow human beings cannot but
affect all of us and be of our concern. The assessment
of human rights in post-Mao China as presented in the
foregoing chapters can be summarized as follows:

A Summary

Human rights in the Western tradition are basically
rights which the individual possesses at birth. They
are protected by law and safeguarded by political participation in government. The personal dignity and freedom of the individual are also made less vulnerable by
the individual's right and ability to earn a living
freely. When this ability seemed precarious at times in
recent history, the scope of human rights was expanded
to include the right to employment and freedom from
want. However, after World War II, Third World
countries have focused on "collective rights" like the
right to self-determination, the right to independence,
and the right to make free use of a country's resources
by its nationals without reference to any impact on
others. Nevertheless covenants written in the United
Nations and ratified by most nations of the world have
consistently provided the guarantee that in asserting
such collective rights the individual's rights as human
beings must in no way be abridged.

Nations subscribing to the communist ideology con-
sider the individual person's rights as "bourgeois"--
necessary only in a society of opposing classes, and
politically useful only for purposes of propaganda and
psychological warfare. There are no human rights per
se; there are only privileges granted by the state which
the state can also withhold or withdraw. Politics is
the process of establishing through class struggle the
dictatorship of the proletariat led by the communist
party; law is the exercise of coercion to maintain that

dictatorship. Rights are what is granted to individuals on the basis of expediency, as a result of demands made by the nature of political and economic problems requiring resolution and the priorities and circumstances the leadership faces. Hence neither law nor individual rights are constant or enduring. This outlook is shared by the Communist Party of China and the government of the People's Republic of China which it controls.

The Chinese tradition, however, did not lay the foundation of such a system. Chinese tradition is humanist, resting on the Confucian concepts of jen (humanity), and i (integrity and moral obligation). It extolls limited government which is justified by a "Heavenly Mandate" that must be earned--and can be just as readily lost--by those who govern; it values harmony and contentment among the people, who in the final analysis must pass on the record of performance. It is a tradition enriched and supplemented by the Buddhist sentiment of compassion and the ancient legalists' insistence on legal codes before which all persons are equal, not to mention Taoism and many other strands of thought. After the overthrow of the imperial system in 1911, revolt against the Confucian tradition was really limited to dissent against its ossified forms and rigidities in society and politics. The fundamental spirit of China's humanist tradition was never denied. During the Nationalist period, Western legal codes were introduced and modernization of the economy began without a social revolution. However, when the Chinese Communist Party gained power in 1949 after a protracted war with Japan that lasted eight years (1937-45) followed by four years of civil war, its approach was totally different. Its Marxist-Leninist ideology was to the Chinese people an imported doctrine alien to China's own tradition and the Chinese Community Party had to create "class struggle" to implement its system.

The political system Mao built was true to the Marxist-Leninist doctrine. Mao began by defining a portion of the nation's population as class enemies upon whom the Communist dictatorship was forcibly imposed. They were used as scapegoats when difficulties arose. Both the government and the military were tools of the Party dedicated to keeping it in power. The armed forces (the People's Liberation Army or PLA) were kept indefinitely on a war-footing in the face of both internal (counter-revolutionary) and external (Western) threats.

After Mao's death, his political system has remained intact. In fact, under Deng Xiaoping, the Communist Party which was decimated during the Cultural Revolution is being restored and transformed into a Soviet-style communist leadership and policy-making organization. "Democratic-centralism" is applied as before. This means that policy decision are made at the

top echelons by the Party Central Committee, but primar-
ily--almost exclusively--by the Politburo and its Standing Committee. While Deng has not assumed all the top
titles in party and government, he holds real power and
is the final decision maker. But he is not without
detractors. The rank and file of the Communist Party
are currently being purged. Deng is treating his opposition in the same was as Mao, and widespread purges
continue.

As a public relations gesture, the original
People's Political Consultative Conference, including
numerous elderly party members and one-time sympathiz-
ers, has been reconvened and some previous Democratic
Parties and "democratic personalities" have been resuscitated. Of somewhat greater significance has been the
revival of the National People's Congress (NPC) to which
a number of intellectuals have been added. The NPC now
meets more frequently and its Standing Committee under
Peng Chen has assumed a higher profile. It has apparently become a major sounding board for new Communist
policies as announced in statements of the leadership
and has been given the privilege of approval of these
policies.

Deng's rule resembles that of Mao in crucial ways.
Mao governed by political drives targeted against
special groups and disposed of his enemies by extra-
legal means. Deng in his "anti-spiritual pollution" and
anti-crime drives has resorted to the same means.
Clearly neither human rights nor rule by law has been
exalted. A facade of something else was created only
because Deng did not rule in this manner during his bid
for power. But there are the same mass meetings to
participate in, more public executions, the same intimidation, the same rush by the intimidated to join in the
condemnation of whatever victim of the moment, and the
same mass fear, arrests, and alienation. The law
against counter-revolutionaries has remained as severe
as before. The new anti-crime drive has added to the
arsenal for social and political control.

The "education through labor" establishment of
forced labor is a principal extra-legal channel Deng has
greatly expanded. Mao used third party criticisms on
wall posters to attack his opponents during the Cultural
Revolution. Deng did the same with dissidents and
critics to get at Hua Guofeng until he succeeded, which
occurred at the end of 1982. In each case free speech
was suppressed when the critics began to appear too
threatening to the instigator, or when power was consolidated. Exercise of human rights signifies weakness on
the part of the leadership. Mao's personality cult
became outrageous in the end. Deng still has a long way
to rival Mao in this regard but is rapidly assuming a
posture of the final arbiter of all things large and
small.

Mao faced factions aligned against him. So does Deng today. But factions within the Party are not the equivalent of opposition parties, mainly because no faction has ever gone to the public for a mandate. Elections, even when held, have been single-candidate elections. If two candidates are presented, which has happened, they are both carefully pre-selected and approved by the leadership.

Given its ideological outlook and unchecked by political alternatives, the communist leadership adopts draconian measures when faced with problems which must be resolved for the Party to stay in power. Accordingly, in adopting harsh policies of anti-religious and anti-"spiritual pollution" actions, the leadership has been completely oblivious of human rights concerns. Compulsory abortion and public regulation of family life which zealots implement top the many abusive measures against women and children that reflect the Party's fundamental amoral doctrine and lack of concern about human needs and desires. Use of extra-legal "education through labor" detentions to tackle dissidents as well as the unemployed is equally revealing of the dominant concern the Communist Party and its leaders have to hold on to its dictatorship at all cost.

In these circumstances, law affords no protection to the individual's rights as they do in the Western legal tradition. In China, law is the weapon of dictatorship, and in the words of the new Chinese law theorists, quoting Marx, "a political party that has won must rely on its weapons to create terror over the counter-revolutionaries in order to maintain its own rule."[1]

For Mao, even communist law that enforced Party dictatorship was too much of a restraint on his freedom of action, and as long as he was in charge, he refused to permit any codification of law that would hamstring his exercise of arbitrary power. The situation has changed under Deng but efforts to introduce communist law have been slow and use of arbitrary power and extra-legal devices has continued.

The most important new laws introduced by Deng are the criminal code of 1979 and commercial legislation related to foreign investment and enterprise in China. In the change from Mao's total arbitrariness to communist law, some legal standards have Party support. But as practice has proven, this is primarily in commercial law.

A crucial questionn to ask in terms of human rights is whether the accused have the right to defense. In the past, denial of guilt would only aggravate the sentence; under the new code, decisions can be appealed and, on paper at least, the appeals court cannot impose sentences harsher than those of the first instance. But in practice this has made little or no difference. Lawyers, a new institution, can assist in the defense of an accused person. But since lawyers have become "workers of the state," they do not defend their charges, who are not their clients, in the Western legal sense.

As other communist rulers like Stalin discovered, communist law too has its inconveniences. Thus, whenever necessary, it is to be modified or disregarded, particularly in political cases. Deng has apparently followed the same course. Among the notable examples in 1983 were speeding up of procedural rules and shortening of the time limit to appeal in capital punishment cases and, in practice, disregard of these rules altogether in immediately carrying out executions. Public announcements of executions have sometimes preceded court announcements. This has been true of efforts to purge the Party of leftists or Maoists.

In the much advertised or otherwise well known cases of court action, the lack of application of announced principles based on the new laws and due process has been patent. The Gang of Four case was a typical political show trial. There was no cross examination of witnesses. The accused were held without trial for several years. In the absence of careful linkage of acts committed against victims to the individual defendants the trial disregarded rules of evidence. The accused were not allowed to have their own lawyers. The procedure used against the dissident Wei Jingsheng were also tendentious and faulty, and based on the characteristic treatment of counter-revolutionaries.

In the great number of cases of arrests and sentences as a result of the crackdown on crime, little is known about court proceedings. It is perhaps significant that regardless of new procedures, of 2,400 known arrests of individuals (see Appendix), fewer than two percent won acquittal. The rest were either found guilty or appear to have been detained indefinitely. (Personal knowledge about some cases indicates that proof of innocence is still a novel experience and supports the statistics about this provided in the Appendix.) Particularly vulnerable to such looseness of procedure are obviously those arrested for political reasons.

Outside the area of prescribed punishment in China's criminal law, there is a much larger domain of detention and punishment under the euphemous categories of "reform through labor" and "education through labor." "Reform through labor" was the original forced labor institution aimed at counter-revolutionaries and was established immediately after the communist seizure of power. It was later merged with the criminal law system. "Education through labor" is an administrative system through which almost anyone can be assigned to a camp against his/her will by anyone in authority. Both systems have been used widely in the past, but "education through labor" is now the principal device to place dissidents, politically and socially undesirable elements and unemployed persons for a period of up to four years in labor camps. Of course, rearrests and reassignments are frequent, making the sentences in practice much longer. These extra-legal measures even outweigh the absence of due process within the legal system in effect so that safeguards under Chinese communist law are really meaningless.

Constitutions accordingly are but a facade behind which basic rights that are proffered on paper are readily withdrawn, modified and ignored. Constitutions themselves multiply as revisions, often quite radical, are made to suit the communist leadership's changing needs. Not counting drafts, thee have been four constitutions since 1949 (1954, 1975, 1978 and 1982), the last two after Mao's death in 1976. All these constitutions contain sections on rights and duties of citizens. The size, formulation and content have varied. The frequent changes and shifts indicate the ease with which Communist Party policy can play with "basic rights." The latest radical revision was Deng Xiaoping's elimination of the stipulation in the 1975 and 1978 constitutions that permitted the use of demonstrations and wall posters as expressions of free speech. In short, one cannot repeat too often that there is no fundamental law that, even if enforced, cannot be readily changed or quickly rescinded. This is, however, to be expected from a system that describes itself as supporting a dictatorship of the proletariat. Whatever his plans for reform, Deng is the head of this system and has not tried to reform or revise it.

Since the real changes in the post-Mao period have been efforts to lift the economy out of the catastrophic state into which it had fallen as a result of thirty years of communist and Maoist mismanagement, a key issue is the impact of economic policies on the rights of individuals. Westerners, including Beijing supporters, sometimes argue that China's new economic policies are proof of a better human rights situation. Some argue that the two are necessarily related. The incentive-inducing measures in agriculture and industry and the greater leeway permitted individual enterprise are clearly beneficial to the individual's freedom of action. As a result of the "responsibility system" and greater decentralization down to the farm level in deci-sion-making affecting production, marketing and special-ization, farm families have benefited and some have greatly increased their income above recent levels. Corresponding policies have been applied to the cities with respect to the licensing of small businesses, most-ly in the service trade, and the substitution of tax payments for surrender of profit to the state. Managers in government enterprises have also been given greater leeway in managerial decision-making such as production, planning, marketing, and personnel policies, especially after Zhao Ziyang's address to the National People's Congress in 1984 advocating the expansion of economic reform to industry. Officially, therefore, getting rich is sanctioned and no longer a "bourgeois" crime. The greater economic freedom, relaxation of controls, and increase in living standards have brought about an improvement in human economic rights. This is what optimists have pointed to as a sign that China may be moving towards democracy because it is moving toward a market economy and the continuing development of the latter could generate in the long run pressure toward greater political rights.

But the system is still based on the assignment of jobs tying people to the kind and place of work, separating families, preventing labor mobility, and, for millions working in reeducation or detention camps, forced labor. Free economic choice is still the exception, not the rule.

As mentioned before, the criminal law has been toughened to offset greater economic freedom. To the limitations on economic rights has been added the worst of all, control of procreation. Under a vigorously enforced one child per family policy the controls include keeping a public record of menstruation of individual women of child-bearing age, assigning the right to procreate by priority, and enforcing compulsory abortion even at the latest stages of pregnancy. With the aid of neighborhood activists, the Chinese Communist Party has thus violated a most intimate aspect of human life and dignity. Family life and human procreation are treated like stock breeding. China does face a most serious demographic problem in the race between population increase and economic growth, but this is a problem that was aggravated or caused by population policies under Mao Zedong. The moral dilemma and alternative policies paying greater heed to human rights are, however, ignored and probably not even seen in their philosophical significance.

Economic improvements lead to rising expectations; an expanding market sector threatens priorities dear to the Communist Party, the bureaucracy and the military. Another problem is that economic reforms create greater income differences and challenge the monopoly of power on the part of lower and middle level Party cadres. There are therefore opponents to such reforms on these grounds. This is a source of instability and may be a factor that will bring to a halt or even reverse the measures that have improved economic rights and conditions. It can be expected to promote more widespread use of political authority to remedy personal grievances or to punish those who have been successful.

The fundamental issue, deeper than all political,

legal and economic problems, is ideological, namely, what people think. What is at stake is communist doctrine versus freedom of thought. Turning against Mao's policies, the new regime has created or at least aggravated the problem of doctrinal sanction of its role without which continuation of communist rule would be impossible to justify. The stronger the belief in Mao's infallibility in the past, the greater the disillusion- ment after the "great helmsman's" fall. The deceived and disillusioned among the former faithful have to be provided with a new belief and hope. The "crisis of confidence" lamented by the new leadership has to be overcome.

PRC leaders have admitted that their past "blind faith" in Mao was "theology," not true Marxism and that the practices of the cult of personality smacked of "feudal superstition." In contrast, the new leaders say, "scientific socialism" has to be reinstituted and followed. So Mao's excesses are gone; but the communist doctrine is to remain. However, Marxism-Leninism is still an alien creed. To give it a Chinese component, the "Thought of Mao Zedong" as a label has been retained, and it allegedly provides the necessary adjustment to the doctrinal "truth" with a Chinese flavor. No substitute has been introduced but Deng's Selected Works are now widely read in China.

In the effort to explain how under a socialist regime the horror of the Cultural Revolution and other atrocities were possible, some of the PRC leaders brought in the Marxist concept of "alienation," an atti- tude of turning away from and negating a principle, which Marx had applied to "bourgeois capitalism." Alienation from socialism was proclaimed as having been the reason for errors committed under Mao, but errors which allegedly did not disprove the basic correctness of the doctrine itself. For Deng Xiaoping this was going too far and the perpetrators of this doctrinal sin had to undergo the same procedure of self-criticism and confession that was standard under Mao. The same has been true for an attempt to find "humanism" in the young Marx, and, therefore, in socialism--which would protect the system against repetition of such grave errors in the future. The irreducible doctrinal foundation of the Chinese communist faith remains the four cardinal principles of Deng Xiaoping: the socialist way, the leadership of the Communist Party, the dictatorship of the proletariat, and Marxism-Leninism and Mao Zedong Thought. If the space has widened for the caged bird, the cage remains. The Chinese Communist Party under Deng has not undergone a real matamorphosis.

Since attempts to resolve the problem of "aliena- tion under socialism" have proven unacceptable to Party leaders, the doctrine of "scientific socialism" has to be strengthened. Perhaps the most extreme attempt of doing that has been the creation of a notion of "spiritual socialism," obviously an attempt to fill the void of the materialistic system that has failed to fulfill its promises even in the area of material well-being. According to Hu Yaobang, "spiritualism," consisting of "five stresses" (decorum, manners, hygiene, discipline and morality), "four beauties," (mind, language, behavior and environment), and "three loves" (party, motherland and socialism), is to fill the void. This Maoist game of numbers is supposed to present a commonly shared belief to take the place of unacceptable "bourgeois thought." Those who dare to disagree and voice alternative propositions are subjected to the drive against "spiritual pollution"--which can end in arrests, or at the very least loss of position and livelihood.

The Chinese Communists' meager offering of spirituality has stepped up the search for true spiritual values by some groups as evidenced in their growing religious activities even though constitutional guarantees of "freedom of religion" have remained largely paper promises. Under the new policy, however, an effort has been made to demonstrate to the rest of the world a more tolerant attitude toward religion. Temples and churches, even seminaries, have been reopened with some fanfare. However, government interference remains and impediments to religious practice are numerous.

For the sake of modernization, intellectuals are courted and their treatment has improved. In many cases they have been co-opted into organizations and positions where jealousy and opposition on the part of Party stalwarts have been evoked. The need for better educated administrators has also led to pursuit of improvements in education. Where this is difficult to provide in China, students in large numbers have been sent overseas--in 1984, 15,000 to the United States alone. Though a very high percentage of these overseas students come from families of privileged echelons, their exposure in the West will inexorably have an impact on the intellectual horizon eventually of China. In the long run these may be latent forces whose effect on the doctrinal straitjacket is unforeseeable.

As in all areas the new regime is torn between the needs of reform, modernization and liberalization and a totalitarian party's political instinct to hold on to ideological sanction and the tools of total power. Human rights are caught in between. Improvements in the immediate years after the death of Mao and the overthrow of the Maoists have largely disappeared as a result of the tightening of control under Deng. Between communist doctrine and power there is no room for individual freedom.

What to Expect?

In assessing post-Mao China from the various per-

spectives in relation to human rights, one comes in each
case face to face with the dilemma between the requirements of modernization and the demands of communist
doctrine and structure. China plainly is at a cross-
roads. Will the Chinese communists be able to make
progress economically, particularly with foreign help?
If so, and if the foreigners insist on a modicum of real
tolerance and respect for human rights, then we may see
in theory a continuation of the present vacillations
between more freedom and tighter control, all within a
basically communist framework.

However, from the communist leaders' point of view,
the Western crutch will eventually have to be removed.
Their hope, of course, is that they will have by then
gained enough in technical knowledge and material benefits to be able to dispense with such outside assistance
and reconstitute and develop a fully communist system.
What this means for human rights is obvious.

Growing dependence on the West would pose a serious
obstacle to such a reversion. Whether the People's
Republic will be able to succeed economically without
the West is a matter of opinion. From a non-communist
perspective, the record of communist systems has been
failure in virtually every realm except military prepar-
edness and what that means to weaker powers, especially
neighbors. The communist record of performance has been
destructive, not constructive. From this point of view,
therefore, it is highly questionable whether the Chinese
will be able to reconcile the fundamentally irreconcil-
able. The communist system does not lend itself to the
efficient use of foreign economic aid even if it should
be forthcoming in such massive quantity as to affect the
balance, which is most unlikely under current world
conditions.

The contradiction between the working of free ideas
and enterprise on the one hand and control and regulation on the other cannot be patched over permanently. A
return to orthodox communist principles would lead to
the old quandary. On the other hand, transition from a
communist, totalitarian system to a truly free system in
terms of intellectual, political, social and economic
order cannot easily occur without violence. For the
sake of China and the future of human rights the hope
must be that under whatever label it will bear, the
Chinese system will find a way toward a truly free
future. How likely is such an outcome?

Fortunately for China, its culture has a strong
tradition of humanity, concern for the individual as
well as justice and righteousness, on which a modern
free society can be built. This tradition contains
respect for individual freedom within a framework of
self-discipline, and a strong sense of mutual obligation. Norms of human ethics, backed by a legal order
and a sense of compassion once provided the basis of

social harmony. If these values can be uncovered from under the over-burden of Maoism and communism, they can serve as guarantee of human rights in a future free Chinese society.

The fate of China is a great concern to the United States and the rest of the world. The reasons go beyond the long historical contacts among educators, missionaries, and businessmen, the romance of the Orient, and the commercial and strategic interests of today and tomorrow. To Americans the cause of human rights in a society of such cultural richness has a special meaning. America has not had a long history of a single cultural origin. Its cultural heritage is derived from diverse sources, joined together by a common search for human freedom, which is the very foundation of human rights. America's heritage is like that of the whole human race. The Declaration of Independence is truly the source not only of nationhood for Americans, but of an international humanism to which the United States has made its contribution. Human rights have been and should by right be a major element of American foreign policy.

However, this policy must be applied wisely. We assume that the basic concepts of freedom are shared in all societies though their applications may vary. There can be no argument about the basic freedoms of thought and beliefs, of speech and of participation in choosing one's economic and political destiny. To guarantee these freedoms other nations do not have to be re-made in America's image. However, the true freedoms must not be sacrificed on the altar of diversity. In our relationship with China, a basic principle must be to encourage the growth of humanist ideas which are part of the true Chinese heritage.

ENDNOTES

1. The purpose of communist law, therefore, is not the
   <u>protection</u> of the individual, but the preservation
   of the Communist Party and system. (Lecture on
   Criminal Law of the Research and Teaching Group on
   Criminal Law of the People's University law faculty,
   March 1982.)

Appendix:
A Statistical Analysis

<u>Explanatory Notes</u>

This appendix attempts to analyze certain quantifiable aspects of the PRC's formal and informal judicial and penal system, including, for example, "education through labor," on the basis of individual cases reported in two national and two provincial newspapers published in the People's Republic of China during the post-Mao years of 1978-83 inclusive. The reader needs to be reminded of the fact that officially sanctioned news on "crime" may be and, we believe, is uneven in reporting and that this unevenness has varied over time. The findings are based on officially sanctioned reports and this fact must be borne in mind. Nevertheless, while the unevenness is likely to reflect the kinds of offenses about which reporting may be permitted, encouraged, discouraged or neglected, a great deal can be learned from these reports on the judicial process in communist China and the manner in which the dictatorship of the Communist Party is upheld.

The analysis focuses on four principal aspects: (1) the nature of the reported offense, (2) the severity of the punishment, (3) the length of time between arrest and sentence and other aspects of judicial procedure, from which additional information can then be derived, such as the proportion of persons held in prisons or labor camps for different offenses probably without trial and/or sentence, and (4) the differential justice meted out to Party versus non-Party members.

Under "nature of offense" reported (for example, in Table 1), the distinct categories adopted are (1) political and ideological--including alleged "counter-revolutionary," spying, religious, "feudalistic-superstitious," and seditious activities; (2) economic--including smuggling, speculation, bribery (both giving and taking of bribes), misappropriation of state and public property, and destruction of the environment and resource base; (3) social order and security--including not only such common crimes as stealing, armed robbery, murder, fraud, white slavery, rape, and mass rioting and killing, but also offenses varying from gambling and immorality to violation of individuals' civic rights and disorderly conduct, and (4) other--including illegal border crossing (mostly to Hong Kong) and offense against the government's birth control and marriage policies.

Under severity of punishment, four categories are used in classification: (1) severe punishment--including the death sentence, the suspended death sentence (normally suspended for two years), and life imprisonment, (2) imprisonment for a fixed term, (3) confinement to "education through labor" detention centers or mobile camps, and (4) all other.

The "case count" is based on the number of individuals accused of having committed the various offenses. The data on hand for 1978 were derived from the official Renmin Ribao (People's Daily); the data for 1979 were derived from the two national papers (Renmin and Guangming) plus one local paper (Nanfang Ribao published in Canton, South China); only the information since 1980 has been derived from four sources (the above three plus the Sichuan Ribao published in Chengdu, Sichuan in Southwest China). Not surprisingly the case counts have increased greatly since 1980, because the national publications are much more reticent on "crime" and punishment, contenting themselves with general reporting on policy matters and some occasional statistics about penal conditions and the judicial system.

The total number of cases we have examined for this Appendix averaged about 500 a year in 1980 and 1981 and about 600 a year in 1982 and 1983. The cases reported in the Canton (South China) newspaper also numbered many times more than those reported in Sichuan. The statistical results may, therefore, appear, prima facie, to be dominated by conditions in Kwangtung.

The 2,369 reported cases in this Appendix do not all contain the data needed. From 1980 to 1983, the usable cases containing the data for analytical purposes were close to 400 a year. Accordingly, the sample size for those years has been relatively constant.

Nature of Reported Offenses

According to Table 1, economic offenses and disturbances of public order and security accounted for an overwhelming number of cases of arrests and punishments reported in the official media. Economic offenses were especially numerous in 1982 when the economic aspect of "spiritual pollution" first received wide attention. Economic offenses were also relatively significant when reporting on all matters of crime and punishment was scarce as in 1978. The high ratio of public disorder and security offenses in all the years--except in 1978 when none was reported--varies from about 40 percent (1980 and 1982) to 54 percent (1983) and 60 percent (1981). In interpreting figures in this category, one should bear in mind (1) that some common crimes have been included in reporting and (2) that disorderly conduct and disturbance of public order are a convenient category into which unemployed and recalcitrant members of the society, including political dissidents, can be conveniently pigeonholed both through the courts and administratively through extra-legal channels for at least four years under the Education through Labor decree of 1957 (republished with supplement in 1979). Finally, annual variations in reporting suggest that the enforcement of criminal law follows the trends set by the Communist Party leadership.

In spite of the numerical dominance of economic and social offenses the reported data of 1981-83 still contained about 10 percent of offenses that are political and ideological. The proportion was higher in the 1978-80 period because reported offenses in the other categories were lower and because, for 1979 and 1980, the data include trials of the "Gang of Four" and other major political figures of the Mao period.

Table 1 also shows that of the accumulated 2,369 cases reported in 1978-83, 1,767 persons have been sentenced whereas 602 have not. The latter constitute 25.4 percent of the total number reported arrested who were held with or without trial, but who had not had their sentences announced. Many were probably held without trial. This ratio rose to 29.2 percent in 1982-83 during the Dengist period.

Cases without Sentence Reporting

Table 2 shows that the number of unreported sentences was higher in 1982-83, distributed principally between the economic and public order categories. There was a large increase in the political and ideological category in 1983. These figures reflected the anti-"spiritual pollution" and anti-crime drives of that period. One possible explanation of the large proportion of such cases without sentence reporting was the use of detention without trial as a means of squashing dissent and opposition.

Severity of Punishment

Table 3 shows the relative severity of punishment meted out to the offenders. Based on the reported 1,767 cases with announced sentences the proportion of those sentenced to "education through labor" institutions has been relatively low. This is open to two different interpretations. First, proportionately fewer cases in this category have been reported than those in the other categories because education through labor is an administrative decision that does not go through the courts. Alternatively, one can assume that the relative

Table 1

Nature of Offenses Reported in PRC Newspapers by Kind

Year	Total Number of Persons*	Political and Ideological	Economic	Public Order	Other
		(Percent)			
1978	7	14.3	85.7	---	---
	(13)	(7.9)	(92.3)	(---)	(---)
1979	101	18.8	8.9	53.5	18.8
	(112)	(20.5)	(8.0)	(54.5)	(17.0)
1980	388	21.6	29.4	39.4	9.5
	(496)	(17.1)	(34.3)	(39.5)	(9.1)
1981	417	8.9	30.0	59.0	2.1
	(542)	(9.0)	(30.3)	(59.0)	(1.7)
1982	418	10.0	51.0	38.3	0.6
	(617)	(7.5)	(52.4)	(39.7)	(0.4)
1983	436	8.7	29.4	59.9	2.0
	(589)	(12.2)	(32.1)	(54.0)	(1.7)
Total	1,767	12.5	33.7	49.5	4.4
	(2,369)	(11.7)	(36.6)	(48.1)	(3.6)

*The numbers in the parenthesis in the "Total Number" Column include persons held but either not yet sentenced or having sentences that are not announced. Therefore, the difference, for example, between 589 and 436 or 153 for 1983, represents persons held without announced sentences.

Table 2

Nature of Offenses in 602 Cases
Without Reported Sentences

Year	Total Number of Persons	Political and Ideological	Economic	Public Order	Other	Total
			(Percent)			
1978	6	---	100.0	---	---	100.0
1979	11	36.4	---	63.6	---	100.0
1980	108	0.9	51.9	39.8	7.4	100.0
1981	125	9.6	31.2	59.2	---	100.0
1982	199	2.0	55.3	42.7	---	100.0
1983	153	22.2	39.9	37.3	0.6	100.0
Total All Years	602	9.1	45.2	44.2	1.5	100.0

Table 3

Percent Distribution of Sentences by Category of

1,767 Persons Arrested as Reported in Table 1

	(Percent)		
Year	Death, Suspended Death and Life Sentence	Term Imprisonment*	"Education through Labor" Institutions	Other
1978	---	14.3	---	85.7
1979	17.8	74.3	---	7.9
1980	16.2	48.5	12.6	22.7
1981	16.1	65.5	8.2	10.3
1982	12.4	63.6	3.3	20.6
1983	25.9	53.4	4.1	16.5

*Including submission to special controls while out on parole.

reporting frequency on education through labor cases is not biased. If this is true, since the actual number of such cases is easily many, many times greater than those included in the present sample, the total number of persons held for offenses against the regime must also be equally a huge multiple of the 2,369 cases gathered here.

Leaving aside the category of "education through labor," a comparison for each year between the percent figures in the first columns under "category of sentence" would show the severity of punishment in the PRC. Thus, in 1983, 25.9 percent of the sentences consisted of capital punishment, suspended death sentences (2-year suspension which may be suspended further or in the most lenient cases commuted to life) and life imprisonment. At 53.4 percent those sentenced to term imprisonment were just about twice in number. The ratio of the most severe sentences was lowest in 1982 (12.4 percent) because of the predominance of economic crimes.

Matching Punishment to Offense

Table 4 relates the two dominant categories of offenses to the sentences. The data very clearly indicate that the public security and disorder offenses were consistently punished with the most severe sentences (death and life) far more frequently than economic offenses.

Regarding term imprisonment, the public order offenses ran a close second to the economic ones except in 1979-80. In the education through labor category, the public order offenses also show a higher proportion than economic offenses. The explanation again seems to lie in the inclusiveness of offenders thrust into this convenient catch-all group.

Can One Ever Win Acquittal?

Table 5 indicates that once arrested in the PRC, the chance of acquittal is exceedingly low. This proportion reached the highest level, only 2.2 percent, in 1981. People arrested are either sentenced or held without sentence, perhaps without trial. The latter category varied from 22 to 32 percent between 1980 and 1983.

Fast Severe Sentences

Table 6 shows the distribution of all those cases, for which the elapsed time between arrest and sentence can be calculated, by length of time elapsed before the pronouncement of sentence and the severity of the sentence. It is apparent for all the sentence categories that in cases where sentences were reported, sentencing took generally less than six months. It is equally apparent that death and other severe sentences

Table 4

Severity of Sentence by Category of Offense

Year	Economic Offenses (Percent)				Public Offenses (Percent)			
	Death, Suspended Death and Life Sentence	Term Imprisonment	"Education through Labor" Institutions	Other	Death, Suspended Death and Life Sentence	Term Imprisonment	"Education through Labor" Institutions	Other
1978	---	---	---	100.0	---	---	---	---
1979	11.1	55.6	---	33.3	31.5	66.7	---	1.9
1980	8.8	33.3	31.6	26.3	26.1	68.0	---	5.9
1981	6.4	75.2	2.4	16.0	22.0	61.0	11.4	5.7
1982	4.2	74.6	1.4	19.7	21.9	60.6	6.3	11.2
1983	8.6	56.3	---	35.1	34.9	55.9	6.5	2.7

Table 5

Disposition of Persons Arrested According to News Media Report

Year	1978	1979	1980	1981	1982	1983
Number of Persons Reported	13	112	496	542	617	589
			(Percent)			
Already Sentenced	53.8	89.3	77.4	74.7	65.6	72.7
Acquitted	0.0	0.9	0.8	2.2	2.1	1.4
No Disposition Reported	46.2	9.8	21.8	23.1	32.3	26.0

Table 6

Percent Distribution of Cases by Length of Pre-trial, Detention, Trial Time and Severity of Sentence

	Detention and Trial Time								
	1 to 3 Months			4 to 6 Months			Over 6 Months		
Year	Death, Suspended Death and Life Sentence	All Other	All Sentences Total	Death, Suspended Death and Life Sentence	All Other	All Sentences Total	Death, Suspended Death and Life Sentence	All Other	All Sentences Total
				(Percent)					
1978	---	---	---	---	---	100.0	---	---	---
1979	46.2	42.6	43.3	30.8	18.5	20.9	23.1	38.9	35.8
1980	56.1	60.2	59.0	19.5	9.2	12.2	23.4	30.6	28.8
1981	50.0	39.9	41.7	25.0	38.5	36.0	25.0	21.7	22.3
1982	48.1	35.6	37.7	40.7	27.4	29.6	11.1	37.0	32.7
1983	60.3	37.5	45.3	20.7	33.9	29.4	19.0	28.6	25.3

were more likely to be handed out within three months of arrest, and that of those receiving such sentences most did within six months of arrest. In 1982 this ratio reached almost 90 percent.

Table 7 presents the same analysis of elapsed time from pre-sentence detention to the pronouncement of sentence, relating it to the nature of offense. The data suggest that economic offenses take more time to reach a definitive sentence than offenses against public order. All other offenses tended to be dealt with quickly except in 1979-80 when there was the show trial of the Gang of Four and other political personalities.

Unreported Dissident and Other Arrests

Wei Jing-sheng and Fu Yueh-hua were the only two dissident cases out of 32 names reported by Spearhead in its No. 19, Autumn 1983 issue which appeared among the 2,369 cases covered in our survey. This gives us some idea of the mass of unreported arrests.

Attorneys at Court?

What role did attorneys play in the 2,369 cases we have examined? In Wei Jingsheng's case, the accused argued on his own behalf, having failed to have the attorney of his own choice. In the Gang of Four trial, Jiang, Yao and Wang defended themselves; Zhang stood mute; the others had government appointed attorneys. In none of the other two thousand plus cases was the presence of any attorney or the presentation of legal arguments ever reported by the media. The official press has carried reports of attorney activities but has been inordinately silent on their court arguments.

Inequality before the Law

Within our sample of the 2,369 persons who were arrested, information is available on 1,869 cases concerning the individual's Communist Party membership or non-membership. Altogether there were 587 Party members and 1,282 non-members. Table 8 shows that for each category of offense the proportion of those given the more severe sentences is consistently higher for non-Party members than for Party members. This is true in the case of life imprisonment and worse (capital punishment and suspended death sentence) and in longer (7 years or more) fixed-term sentences. For instance, of those reported arrests for upsetting public order in the post-Mao years of 1978-83, 29.8 percent of non-Party members were sentenced to death down to life imprisonment. The corresponding proportion for Party members arrested for the same offense and given the same sentences was only 5 percent. Similarly, for non-Party members given sentences from death to life imprisonment who were arrested for political and ideological offenses it was 26.9 percent versus 2.8 percent for Party mem-

Table 7

Percent Distribution of Cases by Nature of Offense and Pre-trial, Detention and Trial Time

(Percent)

Year	Detention and Trial Time											
	1 to 3 Months				4 to 6 Months				Over 6 Months			
	Economic	Public Order	All Other	Total Offenses	Economic	Public Order	All Other	Total Offenses	Economic	Public Order	All Other	Total Offenses
1978	---	---	---	---	---	---	100.0	100.0	---	---	---	---
1979	50.0	36.8	50.0	42.6	---	36.8	4.2	22.1	50.0	26.4	45.8	35.3
1980	22.7	70.1	58.5	59.3	9.1	18.2	2.4	12.1	68.2	11.7	39.0	28.6
1981	18.3	61.8	43.8	47.2	33.3	32.5	31.3	32.7	48.3	5.7	25.0	20.1
1982	7.1	63.4	83.3	36.3	36.5	28.2	8.3	31.0	56.5	8.5	8.3	32.7
1983	13.3	60.2	25.0	45.3	4.4	34.5	75.0	29.4	82.2	5.3	0.0	25.3

Table 8

Severity of Punishment by Category of Offense:
A Comparison Between Party and Non-Party Members
Among the Arrested, 1978-1983
(Number of Persons and in parenthesis Percent of Total)

	Political and Ideological		Economic		Public Order		Other		Total		Total
	Party	Non-Party	Party	Non-Party	Party	Non-Party	Party	Non-Party	Party	Non-Party	Number
Death Sentence	---	19 (18.3)	5 (1.5)	12 (3.4)	1 (1.0)	148 (19.1)	---	2 (4.0)	6 (1.0)	181 (14.1)	187
Suspended Death Sentence	1 (0.7)	4 (3.8)	1 (0.3)	3 (0.9)	1 (1.0)	38 (4.9)	---	---	3 (0.6)	45 (3.5)	48
Life Imprisonment	3 (2.1)	5 (4.8)	---	11 (3.1)	3 (3.0)	45 (5.8)	---	---	6 (1.0)	61 (4.8)	67
Subtotal	4 (2.8)	28 (26.9)	6 (1.8)	26 (7.4)	5 (5.0)	231 (29.8)	---	2 (4.0)	15 (2.6)	287 (22.4)	302
Imprisonment 7 years or longer	10 (7.1)	18 (17.3)	43 (13.0)	73 (20.7)	19 (19.0)	150 (19.4)	1 (6.7)	12 (24.0)	73 (12.4)	253 (19.7)	326
Imprisonment under 7 years	18 (12.8)	29 (27.9)	77 (23.3)	111 (31.4)	25 (25.0)	233 (30.1)	1 (6.7)	27 (54.0)	121 (20.6)	400 (31.2)	521
Subtotal	28 (19.9)	47 (45.2)	120 (36.3)	184 (52.1)	44 (44.0)	383 (49.5)	2 (13.4)	39 (78.0)	194 (33.0)	653 (50.9)	847

(continued)

Table 8 (continued)

	Political and Ideological		Economic		Public Order		Other		Total		Total Number
	Party	Non-Party	Party	Non-Party	Party	Non-Party	Party	Non-Party	Party	Non-Party	
Education through Labor	2 (1.4)	2 (1.9)	---	58 (16.4)	---	58 (7.5)	---	5 (10.0)	2 (0.3)	123 (9.6)	125
Acquittal	1 (0.7)	1 (1.0)	6 (1.8)	9 (2.5)	---	10 (1.3)	---	---	7 (1.2)	20 (1.6)	27
Party* Discipline	92 (65.2)	---	98 (29.6)	---	26 (26.0)	---	11 (73.3)	---	227 (38.7)	---	227
No Sentence Reported	14 (9.9)	26 (25.0)	101 (30.5)	76 (21.5)	25 (25.0)	93 (12.0)	2 (13.3)	4 (8.0)	142 (24.2)	199 (15.5)	341
Total	141 (100.0)	104 (100.0)	331 (100.0)	353 (100.0)	100 (100.0)	775 (100.0)	15 (100.0)	50 (100.0)	587 (100.0)	1282 (100.0)	1869
Total Number	245		684		875		65		1869		

*Including expulsion from the Party, dismissal from Party office, reduction in rank, demerit and warning.

bers. For those arrested for economic offenses, non-Party members sentenced to seven years or longer in prison the percentage was 20.7 as against 13 for Party members. More complete details are given in Table 8.

Conversely, Party members were more often than not let go with a sentence under Party discipline; expulsion being probably the worst in the form of denial of preferential treatment by virtue of Party membership. But the punishment could be as light as a warning or a demerit in the personnel record. Substitution of Party discipline for court sentence reflects the relationship of the Party to the state described in earlier chapters.

Interestingly, while Communist Party members are never in excess of 4 percent of the total population, Table 8 shows a disproportionately large share of those in trouble as Party members. Does this mean that Party members have been unusually prone to committing offense against the communist system? Or has arbitrary power been exceedingly corrupting?